MISSISSIPPI AXE MURDERS

MISSISSIPPI AXE MURDERS

TRAGEDY IN WATER VALLEY

MARK NEAVES

Published by The History Press
An imprint of Arcadia Publishing
Charleston, SC
www.historypress.com

First published 2026

Manufactured in the United States

ISBN 9781467170932

Library of Congress Control Number applied for

I want to dedicate this book to my wonderful wife, Marti, who has stood by my side for twenty-five years. We have shared a lot of laughter and great times together. I love you very much. I also want to dedicate this book to my two children: Riley, twenty, and Emma Kay, twelve. They are the apple of their daddy's eye. I love you both. All three of them have made my life better.

CONTENTS

ACKNOWLEDGEMENTS

This book would not have been possible were it not for Grant Thompson. He is the head of the Water Valley Historical Society and the curator of the Casey Jones Railroad Museum. His help finding newspaper and magazine articles and pictures was vital to the writing of this book. Thank you, Grant, for keeping history alive in Water Valley.

INTRODUCTION

Water Valley, Mississippi, like many small Southern towns, is a place where neighbors still wave from their front porches as people drive by, where a casserole from your neighbor is mandatory when someone is ill or has lost a loved one, and where people still say please, thank you, yes ma'am, and no ma'am. It is a place where visitors can step back in time by walking down Main Street, stopping in Turnage Drug Store to escape the heat, and ordering an old-fashioned ice cream cone or sundae. When they finish cooling down, they can visit the Casey Jones Museum, discover the Mississippi Blues Trail, or go browsing at the local art galleries that showcase talented artists from the area. When August rolls around, they can return to the famous Watermelon Carnival, which draws thousands of visitors to the town each year.

Despite the warmness and nostalgia of the town, for the residents of Water Valley, the memory of May 4–5, 1931, is never far from their minds. It was on that day that W.B. and Mamie Wagner were cut down in their own home, a bloody axe covered in blood, bone, and hair left behind by their murderers. As the search for their bodies began, a dark cloud of worry descended over Water Valley. If the most powerful couple in town could be murdered in the comfort of their home, who was next? Where were the killers, and would they strike again?

If you love true crime and history, join me, author Mark Neaves, as I weave the tale of the formation of Water Valley, the Wagner family, and how two of the most horrific murders in the history of Mississippi turned the town upside down. Using in-depth research and eyewitness accounts, this book allows the reader to walk down the streets of the town and have a bird's-eye view of the crime scene, the search for the Wagners, and the investigation that would eventually lead to the conviction and execution of their killers.

1
A HORRIBLE DISCOVERY

The sun had yet to rise when Callie* Wiggins threw back her covers, sat up on the side of the bed, and stretched. Her muscles woke up slowly as she stood and shuffled across the rough-hewn floors of her house toward her small kitchen. If her feet hadn't been as tough as leather, they would have been full of splinters, but spending her childhood barefoot had created a layer of thick skin on the bottoms of her feet. Staring out the window into the darkness, she smiled, because she loved this time of day before the world woke up. It was a quiet time to read her Bible, sip her coffee, and reflect on the day before her. Unfortunately, she had slept longer than she wanted, meaning she would have to read her Bible later and skip the coffee altogether. Choking down a cold bowl of grits, she chased it with some water, dressed quickly, swept her kitchen, and rinsed out her bowl.

The sun had begun to spill its orange rays over Lee Street as Callie moved down the front steps to stand in her yard. Turning, she looked back at her small home to see whether she had turned out the lights. Her house, number 206, was in what both whites and Blacks in Water Valley referred to as the "Black" part of town. Her small house wasn't much to look at, but it was home, and the rent was affordable for a Black woman who made her living cooking for the elite whites of Water Valley. That morning, May 5, 1931, Callie was headed to the home of W.B. and Mamie Wagner to cook them breakfast, as she did seven days a week.

*Callie Wiggins's name appears on the United States Census Bureau records as Caldonia, but she is named Callie in every newspaper and magazine article researched for this book. She must have preferred to be called Callie.

When she was a girl growing up in Hinds County, Mississippi, her father, Brid* Wiggins, a sharecropper, always enjoyed a good meal when he came home after a long day plowing another man's field. Callie's mother, Sharoltte,** fed him and her children well with what meager supplies she could get her hands on. Callie was taught to cook by her mother and found that she had a talent for it. As she grew, she honed her cooking skills, and on that May morning, like all others, she was grateful to have a place to ply her trade.

Her walk to work was short, only eight-tenths of a mile; despite being so close to her employers' home, her life could not have been more different. Living in Jim Crow Mississippi, Callie's right to eat in white restaurants, use white restrooms, attend white churches, and vote, despite the passage of the Nineteenth Amendment in 1919, didn't exist. If she passed a white person on the streets of Water Valley, she had to avert her eyes and, regardless of their age, address them as "sir" or "ma'am." As with most African Americans living in the South during the 1930s, Callie struggled not only socially but also economically, leaving her and millions of other African Americans living below the poverty line.

323 Wagner Street, W.B. and Mamie Wagner's house, was the picture of wealth, filled with possessions that Callie Wiggins could have only dreamed of. As the president of the Bank of Water Valley, W.B Wagner was the head of the most powerful financial institution in Yalobusha County. He also owned Wagner's Company Clothing, a store that catered to the clothing needs of the residents of Water Valley. W.B.'s success came with power, prestige, and a healthy bank account. In June 1914, the Wagners' wealth was on full display when the *Water Valley Itemizer*, the local newspaper, reported that W.B. and Mamie Wagner had received delivery of a brand-new Mitchell five-passenger touring car from Memphis, Tennessee.

With the Mississippi humidity as thick as fleas on a dog, Callie was covered in a fine sweat by the time she reached the steps that led up to the Wagners'

*Brid Wiggins is listed in the 1910 U.S. Census Bureau records. The spelling of Brid might or might not be correct. Often, the U.S. Census Bureau has several spellings for a person's first and last name. Being that Brid was the consistent first name, we must assume that it is correct.

**Sharoltte Wiggins in listed in the 1910 U.S. Census Bureau records. The spelling of Sharoltte might or might not be correct. Often, the United States Census Bureau has several spellings for a person's first and last name. Being that Sharoltte was the consistent first name, we must assume that it is correct.

A modern view of W.B. and Mamie Wagner's house. *Water Valley Historical Society.*

property. Pausing, she pulled a red bandana from her dress pocket, wiped the sweat from her eyes, and walked up the concrete steps to stand in the front yard. The morning's quiet was interrupted as a cricket chirped out its last song before hopping away to find a cool place to sleep the day away. Reaching the porch, Callie spotted Sam Whitaker, an eighteen-year-old African American part-time chauffeur and yard boy for Mr. W.B. and Ms. Mamie.

Sam Whitaker was small for his age, standing an inch or two shorter than his younger sister Adelle and thin as a rail. That morning, he was wearing a pair of worn overalls that appeared too big for his small frame. His features were also youthful, making him appear as if he had never shaved or needed to. When he stood, he had a habit of resting his left hand on his hip, giving him a look of nonchalance or a devil-may-care attitude. His dark eyes seemed to never stay still, as if his soul wasn't content to be in his body.

As Sam approached Callie, she saw that he was holding a slingshot. "What ya doin' Sam?"*

*The dialogue and how it was recorded as spoken by Sam Whitaker, Emmett Shaw, Adele Whitaker, and Callie Wiggins was taken from an article written by Detective John Fox in *Master Detective* magazine in 1933. Fox was there during the interrogations, and he wrote down the suspects' dialogue in the manner as it is in this book.

His eyes darting back and forth, Sam said, "These jaybirds been eatin' up all Mr. Wagner's cherries in da orchard, thought I would kill a few. What you doin' here?"

"Came to cook the Wagners' breakfast, what you think?" Callie declared.

"Ain't no use fo' you to go in th' house, th' white folks ain't here," Sam declared and then, without a goodbye, turned and walked away.

The kitchen where Callie Wiggins spent so much time cooking for W.B. and Mamie Wagner. *Water Valley Historical Society*.

Ignoring Sam's strange comment, Callie shook her head and turned to the house. The screen door creaked on its hinges as she opened it, reached for the interior door's knob, turned it, and stepped inside. Blinking, it took a moment for her eyes to adjust to the darker interior before she could see the inside of the house.

"Hello," she called out, her voice sounding small and hollow.

No one answered. Maybe they weren't home like Sam said, but in the past, they had always let her know if they weren't going to be home. Walking farther into the house, she noticed signs of a struggle. The furniture, which always stayed in the same position, was overturned and scattered around the living room. "Something ain't right," Callie thought, easing her way to the kitchen. No one, not even Ms. Mamie, knew the kitchen as well as she did. Callie knew where every pot, pan, spoon, sack of flour, bag of sugar, and cup belonged. She also knew which eye on the stove burned the hottest and which spot on the floor would creak before she stepped on it. That morning in "her" kitchen, Callie saw something that chilled her to the bone: drops of blood on the normally pristine floor. Horror filled, she scrambled backward out the door, leaving the screen door banging on its hinges. Running to the neighbor's house, she pounded breathlessly on their door.

2

THE WAGNER FAMILY COMES TO AMERICA

Yalobusha, the county where Water Valley is located, is a Native American word meaning "tadpole place." The land was originally inhabited by the Cherokee and Choctaw. It was taken by the U.S. government when the Choctaw signed the Treaty of Dancing Rabbit Creek in September 1830. Three years later, on December 23, 1833, the Mississippi State Legislature made Yalobusha an official county. The newly formed county was nine hundred square miles and consisted of twenty-five townships.

Three days before Easter in 1834, the county board met and named the town of Coffeeville as the county seat. The town, whose population was around six hundred in 1834, had been named after General John Coffee, a close friend of General Andrew Jackson, who fought alongside him during the Creek Wars and the Battle of New Orleans.

A year after Coffeeville was named the county seat, future president James K. Polk, while serving as the Speaker of the House, purchased 920 acres in Yalobusha County with his brother-in-law Silas Caldwell. After James Polk's birth in Mecklenburg, North Carolina, in 1795, his family migrated to Tennessee, where his father, Samuel, acquired 8,000 acres before his death in 1827. As the oldest child, it was left up to James, who was thirty-two years old at the time, to divide his father's 8,000 acres and the fifty-three slaves between himself, his siblings, and his mother.

Hoping to take advantage of the success of other Mississippi planters, James and Silas sent twenty slaves—eight children and twelve adults—south to Mississippi from Tennessee to begin clearing their newly acquired acreage. With cotton being "king" in Mississippi, it didn't take long for the Polk Plantation to earn a profit. As the money rolled in, the number of slaves on the plantation continued to rise until there were thirty-four in 1840. Regardless of the plantation's success, Polk was so busy with politics that he rarely came to Mississippi to check on its progress. Trusting his brother-in-law, Polk allowed Silas to run the plantation and turned his attention toward his 1844 presidential bid.

General John Coffee, veteran of the Battle of New Orleans, is the namesake of Coffeeville, Mississippi. *Library of Congress.*

The 1844 presidential election was the fifteenth quadrennial in America and a highly contested election between James K. Polk and Henry Clay. Both men had served as Speaker of the House and were as politically connected as any two men in the United States. Running as a Democrat, Polk narrowly won the popular vote with over 39,000 votes more than his opponent. He also captured 170 of the 275 electoral votes, securing him the office as the eleventh president of the United States of America.

With large issues, such as the annexation of Texas and whether slavery should be allowed in the territories, Polk had his work cut out for him when he was sworn in on Tuesday, March 4, 1845. One of the promises he made when he entered office was that he would serve only one term as president, and when his term was up, he kept his promise by retiring to his home in Nashville, Tennessee, in 1849. Unfortunately, he died of cholera just four months into his retirement. The day he died, Polk Plantation was home to fifty-six slaves and had become one of the most profitable plantations in Yalobusha County.

The town of Water Valley was established in 1834, and for the first decade, the small settlement consisted of only a small group of cabins. As the settlement continued to grow, it was christened Water Valley in 1847. Throughout the rest of the 1840s, the small town expanded, and businesses sprang up along Main Street. Quickly, Water Valley acquired a stagecoach depot, a doctor's office, and several dry goods stores. However, it wasn't until 1852, when the Mississippi Central Railroad was chartered, that Water

Valley began to boom. Once completed, the railroad ran from Jackson, Tennessee, south to New Orleans, carrying cotton to the Gulf of Mexico, where it would be loaded aboard ships and transported to the textile mills of Great Britain. The railroad, which passed through Water Valley, made the town a hub of activity, and soon the community added a drugstore, a hotel, and several churches. With the population increasing, Water Valley incorporated in 1858.

In 1860, with the railroad complete, Water Valley became the headquarters of the Mississippi Central Railroad. As the town grew, talk of secession burned through the Southern states like wildfire. Abraham Lincoln was elected president in November 1860, and South Carolina seceded from the Union in December. Determined not to be left behind, Mississippi seceded, followed by nine other Southern states. With the formation of the Confederate States of America, war was on the horizon, and Jefferson Davis, president of the Confederate States of America, called for 100,000 volunteers from across the South to join the Confederate forces. Filled with fervor for the South, many of the men from Water Valley answered Jefferson's call, mustering for a war that they believed would last only a few short months.

Among the volunteers from Water Valley were brothers William B. Wagner and Daniel R. Wagner, who had migrated from Pennsylvania to Mississippi to establish their fortunes. Their parents, Andrew and Catherine Wagner, had immigrated to the United States from Germany in 1828. The couple were two among six million German immigrants who crossed the Atlantic Ocean between 1820 and 1920. Andrew and Catherine's reason for coming to America has been lost to history; however, many Germans during this period listed their reasons for immigrating as political unrest, religious conflict, and a lack of economic prospects in the motherland. Whatever the Wagners' reasons for leaving, it must have been serious, because as they made their way up the gangplank to the ship, Andrew was holding the hand of their six-year-old son, Andrew P. Wagner, and Catherine was nine months pregnant.

Crossing the deck of the ship, the small family paused and looked at their homeland one last time before descending below deck into the bowels of the ship. Sometime during the choppy fifteen-day trip, Catherine went into labor, giving birth to their second child, a girl named Helena. As the ship pulled into the harbor, Catherine, weakened by childbirth and swaddling her newborn baby, made her way to the top deck, a sense of relief washing over her as she spotted the American shoreline. God is good, she thought, as she kissed newborn Helena and pulled young Andrew close. As they exited the ship, they were lined up by American officials, their papers inspected. They were questioned and subjected to a doctor's exam. Those who were found seriously ill or deemed unacceptable were loaded back onto the ships and sent back across the Atlantic. Andrew, Catherine, little Andrew, and Helena were all approved and released under their own recognizance into the new world.

Like most immigrants, Andrew and Catherine hoped to carve out their American dream. It must have been difficult, being so far from home, being unable to speak English, and having few, if any, prospects. Traveling to Freeport, Pennsylvania, the couple established their new life in the still unincorporated borough. Located on the Allegheny River, Freeport had been settled in 1797 by James McCormick.

By the time the Wagner family arrived in Freeport, construction had been completed on the Pennsylvania Canal, which connected Philadelphia and Pittsburgh. The new construction and increased traffic along the Allegheny River caused Freeport to prosper, and in 1833 the town was incorporated. That same year, the citizens of Freeport went to the polls and elected Jacob Weaver as a burgess, James McCall as an assistant burgess, and other officials. On May 10, 1833, the new officials met, rolled up their sleeves, and began to work at establishing local laws.

As the town grew, so did the Wagner family. Census records show that Catherine gave birth to seven more children by 1846. Unfortunately, Catherine died in 1849 at the age of forty-four. Her death left Andrew, forty-nine, a widower with five young children under the age of seventeen. The youngest, Henry, was three years old at the time of his mother's death. With so many young children living at home and their father having to work to support his large family, the older children were left to raise their younger siblings. No records exist about whether Andrew ever remarried, but he did become a U.S. citizen in 1864. His citizenship came because of the Naturalization Act of 1802, which required an immigrant to be a resident of the United States for five years, give three years notice of his or her intent to naturalize, swear or affirm support of the Constitution, renounce their previous citizenship, demonstrate good moral character, and renounce all titles of nobility.

For many families, the War Between Brothers, as the Civil War was often called, was just a euphemism. For Andrew Wagner's children, it was a harsh reality: Phillip and Henry donned the blue of the Union army while D.R. and William wore Confederate gray. It is unclear what unit

Phillip and Henry joined, but it is possible that it was either the 47th or the 104th Pennsylvania Infantry. William and D.R.'s records clearly state that they both enlisted in the 15th Mississippi Infantry. The 15th Mississippi Infantry consisted of men from Holmes, Choctaw, Quitman, Montgomery, Yalobusha, and Grenda Counties. Sending four sons to war must have been horrific for Andrew Wagner. Fortunately for him and his family, all four of his sons survived the war.

Having engaged in a few skirmishes, it wasn't until April 6–7, 1862, that the 15th Mississippi would be baptized by fire at the Battle of Shiloh in Tennessee. The Battle of Shiloh was the first time many of the untested Confederate and Union soldiers would "see the elephant," a euphemism for engaging in battle for the first time. Until the Battle of Shiloh, Unionists and Confederates alike were overly confident that the war would be won quickly, but Shiloh's 23,746 casualties proved just how long and bloody the Civil War would become. General Ulysses S. Grant wrote in his memoirs, "Up to the battle of Shiloh, I, as well as thousands of other citizens, believed that the rebellion against the Government would collapse suddenly and soon, if a decisive victory could be gained over its armies. After Shiloh, I gave up all idea of saving the Union except by complete conquest." Grant's statement was prophetic, because that is exactly what it took for the United States to win the Civil War, complete and utter conquest of the Confederate army.

D.R. Wagner survived the Civil War to become a highly successful businessman and lived to the age of seventy-five. *Water Valley Historical Society.*

There is no record of what happened to William Wagner at the Battle of Shiloh or what he witnessed, but it was recorded that D.R. was wounded when a piece of artillery shell struck him in the ankle. Later during the war, D.R. was captured by the Union forces; taken to Alton, Illinois; and placed in a prisoner of war camp. Fortunately for him, he was able to escape and make his way to Vicksburg, Mississippi, where he rejoined his unit.

In November 1864, with the Confederacy crippled and close to the end, General John Bell Hood was determined to take Nashville, Tennessee, hoping to turn the Confederacy's fortunes around. He met strong resistance on November 29 when he clashed with Union General John M. Schofield's forces at the Battle of Spring Hill. It was during that battle that D.R. Wagner was wounded yet again. By the time the Confederacy surrendered in April 1865, D.R. Wagner had spent two and a half years in the infantry and eighteen months in the Confederate cavalry, having reached the rank of corporal. When the war ended, William held the rank of quartermaster sergeant.

With the war over, the brothers returned home to Water Valley, but it looked much different than before they left in 1861. Late in 1862, General Ulysses S. Grant and his Union forces happened across the small boom town as they were marching toward Vicksburg to try to secure access to the Mississippi River. If Grant succeeded in taking Vicksburg, he could separate Arkansas, Louisiana, and Texas from the rest of the Confederacy. The strategy was part of General Winfield Scott's Anaconda Plan, which he hoped would squeeze the life out of the Confederacy.

Because of the strategic railroad line in Water Valley, Grant and the Union army settled there to rest and regroup before marching to Vicksburg. During the occupation, Grant's soldiers were allowed to pillage the town and surrounding area for food and other supplies. As was his custom, Grant never let his men spiral completely out of control, but when they left, his army was restocked and rested, and the Mississippi Central Railroad had been destroyed. Fortunately, the railroad was repaired shortly following the war, and its repair shop was moved from Holly Springs to Water Valley, which brought hundreds of jobs to the town.

3

A BLOODY AXE

When Callie Wiggins reached a neighbor's house, she pounded on their door until someone jerked it open to see a wide-eyed, panic-stricken young Black woman panting for air. It is unclear what neighbor Callie sought out, but whoever it was rushed to the phone and called the Yalobusha County Sheriff's Office. Handing the young cook a glass of water, the unknown good Samaritan tried their best to calm her down while they waited for Sheriff C.T. Doyle and City Marshal Leonard Redwine to arrive. Both men were experienced lawmen who held the trust of not only the people of Water Valley but also the citizens of Yalobusha County.

Eleven years earlier, in May 1920, the *Vidette*, a newspaper printed in Iuka, Mississippi, reported how then–City Marshal C.T. Doyle led a U.S. marshal named Whitehead on a successful raid of 60 gallons of alcohol. The article also stated that during the raid an unnamed African American was arrested on bootlegging charges. Later that same month, Doyle was involved in what the press called "one of the most destructive raids to the illicit whiskey manufacturing interests of Yalobusha County" when he led Chief Deputy Marshal C.E. Sisk, Mayor E.E. Temple, and Prohibition agent G.W. Whitehead on a raid of two stills, one twelve miles east of Water Valley and the other fourteen miles southeast of town. The two raids netted 1,500 gallons of whiskey and two prisoners, one white man, Andy Miller, and one Black man, Simon McDonald. Both men were taken to the federal court at Oxford, Mississippi, to be arraigned.

Their bond, which was handed down by Commissioner Smith, was $1,000 apiece. The two 80-gallon copper stills were vigorously smashed with axes and placed in front of the federal courthouse. The message was clear: Prohibition was here to stay, and bootleggers would be subject to the harsh arm of the law.

On the morning he was summoned to W.B. Wagner's home, Sheriff Doyle was a sixty-six-year-old widower who lived at 208 Clay Street in Water Valley. His wife, Ella Doyle, died in 1918 at the age of forty-five after an unsuccessful surgery at Lucky Brinkley Hospital in Memphis, Tennessee. According to an article in the *North Mississippi Herald*, Ella's life had been a shining example of kindness, courage, and Christian faith. She and Sheriff Doyle's marriage had produced five children, one having died in infancy. Their son Lieutenant George Doyle was serving in France at the time of his mother's death and sadly was unable to attend her funeral. Over her twenty-seven years of marriage, Ella had learned to live with the uncertainties, the worry, and the sleepless nights that came with being married to a police officer. Time had not dulled Sheriff Doyle's senses, and at sixty-six he was still as strong as men half his age, with keen eyes and a razor-like attention to detail.

City Marshal Leonard Redwine was twelve years younger than Sheriff Doyle, but he too held the trust and respect of the people of Water Valley. Before being elected city marshal, he had served as night marshal for the town for two months. Like Doyle, Marshal Redwine put his foot down while enforcing Prohibition laws. In 1923, Redwine, while on patrol, spotted Bernard Shipp, a young man, drinking "hooch" from a bottle while standing in Frank Walson's garage. Shipp, catching sight of Redwine, shoved the bottle of white liquor in his pocket quickly, but when Redwine searched Shipp, he found the liquor. Facing a heavy fine or possible jail time, Shipp claimed he had no money and promised Redwine that he would work for the city if the marshal wouldn't officially charge him with a crime. Agreeing to the terms, Shipp left but later failed to report for his duties. After several months, Shipp was arrested and taken before Judge Young. Securing counsel, Shipp requested a trial by jury, but in the end, he was sentenced to $300 and $17.60 in court costs.

As beloved as he was in the county, the press was not always kind to Marshal Redwine, as was evident in August 1923, when the *North Mississippi Herald* ran a scathing article about Night Marshal Redwine's arrest of a young man who was freighthopping. The article also bashed Judge J.W. Young, who sentenced the young man to serve on a convict gang for fifty-eight days. According to the article, there was little evidence that the young man had been trying to ride the rails for free. Reporter D.A. Higdon, in his article about the incident, asked, "Whether the boy is guilty of train riding or not, is it justice to give a boy who is trying to go home 58 days on the convict gang?" The article also stated that Judge Young had spoken to other towns in the surrounding area and found out that they did not prosecute young men for freighthopping, but the railroad expected it of him. Reporter Higdon wrote, "Oh not for justice, but for the railroad." When Higdon told Judge Young that an article about this injustice would be in the newspaper, Young said, "I do not care. I do not plan on seeking office again."

Their voices boomed in unison as Redwine and Doyle ordered their deputies to keep the crowd away from the house. Walking down the sidewalk to the Wagners' home, they paused at the bottom of the concrete steps; Sheriff Doyle pulled his pocket watch from his vest and made a mental note of the time. If this was a murder, which he suspected, he wanted to do everything by the book. Climbing the concrete steps, Doyle and Redwine saw that Callie had left the front door wide open. The screen door, which closed automatically, was the only barrier between the lawmen and the inside of the house. Stepping onto the porch, Sheriff Doyle cupped his hands around his face and peered through the screen door. Unable to see anything, he opened the door and stepped inside. The brightness of the morning sun contrasted so greatly with the interior of the home, it took a minute for the lawmen's eyes to adjust to the dim interior of the house.

When their eyes focused, they eased into the house. Both men, having been hunters most of their lives, instantly recognized the strong, coppery scent of blood. Exchanging a worried glance, their eyes searched every inch of the interior for clues. As political officials, both men had been into the Wagners' home on several occasions and both knew that Mamie was fanatical about keeping a clean house, but today the furniture was overturned and blood splattered the normally pristine floors. In an interview about the murders, Sheriff Doyle said, "In my first examination of this room, I knew that nothing short of murder would have wrought the havoc that was evident in this quiet home. But I was at first puzzled by the absence of the victim."

The farther they moved into the home, the heavier the blood was on the hardwood floors. Several pools of blood had been smeared, leading Sheriff Doyle and Marshal Redwine to believe that the murderer was attempting to clean up the crime scene but had failed miserably. Entering

This is behind the home of W.B. Wagner, where his body was hastily buried beneath rubbish and loose dirt. *The Master Detective magazine.*

the bedroom, they spotted bloody footprints all over the floor. Examining them closely, they agreed that the footprints belonged to a male, but who? As horrific as the scene was, there was still no sign of a body or bodies, but it was clear to everyone that a homicide had taken place, perhaps two. Sheriff Doyle and Marshal Redwine ordered everyone out of the bedroom, fearing that the crime scene might be contaminated. Making their way to the dining room, they were met by other signs of distress. The dining room table and chairs were overturned, and in one corner of the room lay an axe. If they weren't sure a murder had taken place before, they were now, as the axe was covered in blood, hair, and bits of bone.

"No one touches the axe until it is dusted for prints," Sheriff Doyle ordered.

As the deputies secured the crime scene, a loud rumble rose from the crowd outside the home. Rushing outside, Sheriff Doyle saw the crowd digging with their bare hands next to a pepper plant in W.B.'s backyard garden. In a matter of minutes, they had unearthed the body of W.B. Wagner. Two of the men in the crowd grabbed the banker's body and lifted it from the shallow grave. Easing his body back down, the two stepped away while others stepped forward for a closer look.

After examining the body, Sheriff Doyle was convinced that W.B. Wagner had died from injuries caused by the axe found in the dining room. Just above W.B.'s left ear, his head had been turned into a pulp. The right side of his forehead was also caved in, possibly from the blunt side of the axe. There was a long cut from the right side of his forehead that traveled across his face to his left cheek. Bone from his cheek gleamed white in the early morning sun. The crowd, some queasy, some in shock, fell silent as they stared down at the once pillar of the community. The question now was, "Where is Mamie Wagner and is she still alive?"

4

THE WAGNER FAMILY EXPANDS

While working for the railroad as a ticket agent in Water Valley, William Wagner Sr. married Calista Young on December 3, 1860. Calista's father, Dr. John Young, was a prominent physician in Water Valley who also fought for the 15th Mississippi during the Civil War. Whether intentional or not, William's marriage to Calista improved his social standing. Unfortunately, Calista died due to childbirth complications just one month shy of her and William's first anniversary. Their newborn daughter also passed away and was buried with her mother.

Calista's tombstone was inscribed:

Calista Caroline
Wife of
W.B. Wagner
Died
November 3rd, 1861
Aged 21 Years
7 MO'S and 9 D'YS
Also their Infant
Daughter
Aged 7 Days

The grief of losing his wife and first child must have been almost more than Willam could bear, but he threw himself into the war and returned stronger and more determined than ever to carve out a place for himself in the world.

Before the war, D.R. Wagner worked for the McFarland Company in St. Louis, Missouri, buying supplies for plantations and transporting them back to Water Valley. Along with his brother, he decided to make Water Valley his home. Returning from the war as hardened veterans, the brothers determined never to depend on anyone else for employment, so they opened their own business. Whether it was their past work experience or the need for a clothing store in town we might never know, but the brothers opened the W.B. Wagner & Bro. Store. The department store, which was eventually renamed Wagner & Company, quickly became a staple in Water Valley, leading to the Wagner family becoming one of the richest and most powerful families in Yalobusha County.

Despite his role as a Union soldier during the war, Henry Wagner reunited with his brothers by moving, along with his wife and three children, to Water Valley. His son Edward P. Wagner was born shortly after they moved to town. Whether people in the small town viewed him as a carpetbagger is unknown, but his service to the Union possibly caused him some grief in a town that was still fiercely loyal to the fallen Confederacy. In an 1870 census, Henry's profession was listed as a store clerk, which leads us to conclude that he was either working for his brothers or a partner in their new venture.

As a young widower with no children and a drive for success, William would have been a sought-after romantic prospect for the young women of Water Valley. However, possibly still grief-stricken or affected by his wartime experience, he remained single until June 1866, when he married twenty-three-year-old Mary E. Buford. Mary, the second oldest of five children, was the daughter of A.G. and Esther Buford. Mary's father, A.G., originally from South Carolina, was listed as a farmer with an estate valued at $32,195 in the 1860 census. His property also included thirty-three slaves, whom he used to run his farming operation.

Following in William's footsteps, D.R. married on November 1, 1867. His bride, Maria Gertrude Young, was the fourth child of Dr. John Young, his brother William's former father-in-law. Gertrude, as she was called, was nineteen at the time of their nuptials, and D.R. was twenty-seven. As the couple settled into their new lives, their clothing store became a staple in the growing town. Through William and D.R.'s marital connections and their work ethic, they were soon bombarded with business by some of the most affluent citizens in town. More business meant more money, and money meant power.

As Mississippi approached its hottest month, August, William grew nervous and excited as Mary grew larger with their child. With his first wife's and daughter's deaths shortly after birth, William's mind was racked with worry as his wife's due date drew near. In August 1867, the couple's wishes and prayers were answered when Mary gave birth to a healthy baby boy. They named their son William Buford Wagner Jr. in honor of his father. Relief washed over William as he held his son for the first time, unaware that his squirming, red-faced baby boy would meet such a horrible end in May 1931.

As their business grew, so did their family, and in 1869, Mary was pregnant for the second time. With the successful birth of W.B. Jr., William and Mary were overly excited at the prospect of adding another child to their budding family. However, the best-laid plans often fail, and on May 5, 1869, William passed away, leaving his pregnant wife a widow and his children fatherless. His cause of death is unknown, but he was only thirty-six when he died. Just two months later, in July, Mary gave birth to their second child, Andrew Gallatin Wagner. The day of his birth must have been bittersweet for the widowed Mary as she welcomed a healthy child into the world but was saddened that his father had not lived to witness his birth.

The Wagner family grew even larger that same year when D.R. and Maria welcomed their first child, John Henry Wagner. Over the next thirteen years, the couple would add five more children. These six children would grow up in a home unlike the childhood home of their father, uncles, and aunt. Their home was a home of prosperity without worry about where or if their next meal was coming. In simple words, it was a life of privilege. Regardless of their prosperity, D.R. and Maria emphasized the need for their children to work and pull their own weight in the world.

Despite how well things were going for Water Valley and the Wagner family, life in the budding town came to a halt in July 1878.

Upon inspection of a recently arrived tugboat, Vicksburg officials found that most of the crew were dead, and the others were so weak that they could not function. Scared but willing to do the "Christian" thing, many of Vicksburg's residents boarded the tugboat to remove the dead for burial. They also removed the sick crew members and tried to nurse them back to health. In less than a month after the tugboat had docked, yellow fever had claimed the lives of 1,500 residents of Vicksburg. Things only got worse as the epidemic began to spread throughout the rest of the state at an unprecedented rate.

Yellow fever, or Yellow Jack as it was often called, is caused by the bite of an insect that carries the arbovirus. The main culprit of the yellow fever epidemic was the mosquito, the deadliest insect in history. Scientists estimate that mosquitoes have been responsible for the death of around 52 billion people. Mosquitoes can infect animals and humans with over ten different types of deadly diseases.

The symptoms of yellow fever include muscle pain, fever, headache, loss of appetite, nausea, and vomiting. For a small percentage of those suffering from yellow fever, it can be deadly, resulting in such a high fever that their kidneys and liver shut down. The fever's name comes from the jaundiced skin color that people exhibit when they enter the final, toxic stage of the disease. The toxic stage lasts seven to ten days, is unbelievably painful, and often results in the death of the infected.

As the epidemic spread, residents of Water Valley began to take precautions to avoid the dreaded disease. In September 1878, H.W. Freeman reported on Water Valley in the *Memphis Daily Appeal*, stating, "We have ten new cases of yellow fever reported today; only six deaths so far." He also wrote about Drs. Dickson, Smith, and Gant, all of whom were sick with yellow fever or whose relatives were sick, hindering them from being on the front lines during the epidemic. In late September, Dr. J.G. Davis of Lincoln, Nebraska, arrived in Memphis, Tennessee, only to be sent to Water Valley to help the struggling town. When the epidemic ended, around 70 of Water Valley's citizens had died. The death toll was devastating, but it paled in comparison to that of Grenada, Mississippi, which lost 350 of its citizens including the mayor, the sheriff, and all the aldermen in the town of 2,500 residents.

In a letter to Mississippi Governor John Marshall Stone, the Grenada Relief Committee wrote, "Our sheriff and city marshal are dead or gone. Our mayor is dead…our population is reduced to the sick, the doctors, nurses, and undertakers—our people have generally fled the city."

During the 1878 epidemic, there were around 120,000 cases of yellow fever and 20,000 deaths, making it one of the deadliest yellow fever outbreaks in American history. When the epidemic ended, the citizens of Water Valley presented Dr. J.G. Davis with a medal for his excellent care. The medal was inscribed, "Presented to J.G. Davis, volunteer Howard physician, by the citizens of Water Valley, Mississippi, for his noble, untiring, and proficient work among our yellow fever sufferers. Water Valley, Mississippi, 1878." With the epidemic behind them, Water Valley's population continued to soar, and by 1880 there were 2,200 residents living within the town.

5

DETECTIVE FOX

The morning of the murders, Private Detective John J. Fox woke up early, fixed a cup of coffee, and headed to his office in the Columbian Mutual Tower on North Main Street, Memphis, Tennessee. The tower (now named Lincoln-American Tower) was the brainchild of Lloyd Binford, president of the Memphis branch of the Columbia Mutual Insurance Company. When the tower was completed in 1924, it was one of the first internal steel skeleton buildings in Memphis. At twenty-two stories tall with Gothic architecture, covered in white terra-cotta, it rose above the city like an old sentinel guarding the city, its people, and the powerful Mississippi River.

Arriving at the tower, Detective Fox, briefcase in hand, stood staring appreciatively at the building looming over him. Its sleek corners and bright windows appealed to him. With his free hand, he buttoned his double-breasted suit coat, opened the door, and strolled inside. When his eyes adjusted to the darker surroundings, the lobby reminded him of a beehive, with people rushing around in that early morning panic that is a common theme for many employees. Seeing them panic made him glad that he worked for himself. The floors of the lobby, the walls, and even its pillars were constructed from gold-veined Tennessee marble, which shone brightly in the overhead lights. His shoes clicked loudly against the marble as he crossed the lobby to stand in front of the ornately decorated elevator.

"Good morning," Fox muttered, nodding to the others who waited for the elevator.

When the elevator door opened, he shuffled aboard and stared at the ceiling until the elevator reached his floor. It was 8:10 a.m. when he stepped from the elevator and entered the side door to his personal office. Sitting in his desk chair, he shuffled through the large stack of papers, including mail, piled on his desk. He had only just sat down when the main office door opened and his secretary barged inside.

"Mr. Eugene Wagner is waiting in the reception room and wishes to see you," she said, placing a pencil behind her ear.

"Show him in," Fox said.

Eugene Wagner, an influential Memphis businessman, entered the office, his hat in hand, his face pale and painted with worry.

"Good morning," Fox said.

Dispensing with niceties, Wagner said, "My uncle W.B. Wagner, president of the Bank of Water Valley and owner of Wagner Department Store, was murdered last night at his home in Water Valley. The first news of the tragedy was telephoned to me a few minutes ago. His wife is missing, and I fear that something terrible has happened to her!"

At that revelation, Detective Fox sat straight up in his chair and asked, "What were the circumstances surrounding the murder?"

Wagner replied, "I was given only meager details, but I learned from the telephone conversation that my uncle was found in a crude grave and that he has been hacked to death with an axe."

The view from the Columbia Mutual Tower in February 1937. The Mississippi River is pictured here before the levees were built to control the mighty river. *The Commercial Appeal newspaper.*

A young Mamie Wagner many years before her brutal death in May 1931. This is the only portrait of her known to exist. *Water Valley Historical Society.*

A silence fell over the office as Detective Fox processed the grisly information. As a detective, Fox's mind raced through possible motivations for the murder. He also wondered, "Where was Mamie Wagner? Is she alive or dead?" Not knowing the Water Valley couple, he didn't want to make any assumptions, but in his experience, there were several motives for murder. In this case, like all the others he had investigated, he would not assume anything until he had all the facts.

Nodding, Fox said, "We will start for Water Valley immediately." Reaching onto his desk, Fox pressed a buzzer that summoned Captain W.F. Wattam, whom he referred to as a crack operative. Wattam, like Detective Fox, had worked in Memphis and was no stranger to homicide.

With time being of the essence, the trio rushed downstairs, jumped in a car, and blazed their way out of Memphis toward Water Valley. Captain Wattam, who was behind the wheel, pushed the car to around seventy miles per hour for the eighty-seven-mile trip. The men talked little as they zoomed by the cotton and cornfields that dominated the landscape.

Pulling into Water Valley, Wattam slammed on the brakes and came to a screeching halt in front of the Yalobusha County Courthouse, which had been built in 1896. The original design for the courthouse was two stories, with a large clock tower that hovered above the town, ensuring that people knew exactly what time it was at all hours of the day or night. Unfortunately, in 1912, a fire ravaged the building, leaving the town and the county scrambling for a place to reign down justice on criminals. In 1913, the county employed P.J. Krouse, a prominent Mississippi architect, to restore the courthouse. Krouse's design added a third story to the building, topped by a heavy cornice and a large window with Tuscan columns behind a balcony above the main entrance.

Running up the courthouse steps, Fox burst through the doors and asked if he could see the sheriff. A receptionist informed him that the sheriff was at the crime scene and had no intention of returning anytime soon. If he wanted to see the sheriff, he would find him on Wagner Street. Jumping back into the car, Fox allowed Eugene Wagner to guide them through the streets of Water Valley until they turned onto his uncle and aunt's street.

Pulling alongside the curb, Wattam placed the car in park, and they slowly stepped from the vehicle. Pushing through the crowd, Fox, Eugene Wagner, and Wattam climbed the concrete steps until they stood on the large sweeping porch. Stepping inside the house, they were greeted by the grim faces of Sheriff Doyle and Marshal Redwine. Sheriff Doyle, knowing Eugene, quickly filled them in about the morning's events.

Sheriff Doyle then led the three men to the Wagners' bedroom and watched as they took in the scene in wide-eyed horror. The blood, which had been bright red when the sheriff arrived, was now congealing into a dark brown. Leaving the bedroom, they proceeded to the dining room, where Sheriff Doyle pointed out the axe that had been used to kill Wagner.

A current picture of W.B. and Mamie Wagner's bedroom where Sheriff Doyle, despite there being no bodies, became convinced that a murder had taken place. *Water Valley Historical Society.*

The garage no longer stands, but this is the location where the Wagners' bloody car was found, leading law enforcement to believe that Mamie Wagner had also been murdered. *Water Valley Historical Society.*

Bloodstained and still, the axe seemed to present no more danger than one of the wooden spoons in Mamie Wagner's kitchen.

As they stepped outside, Detective Fox asked, "Have you established a motive for this crime?"

Gazing around the scene, Chief Redwine said, "At first we thought it was robbery, but the prosperous status of the victim is the only thing so far to support the theory."

Sheriff Doyle added, "Nothing is missing from the home so far as we can tell and yet there is no other angle to explain what has happened."

Determined to gather every clue, the investigators searched the house repeatedly until they were convinced that no stone had been left unturned. When the fingerprint expert arrived, Sheriff Doyle and Detective Fox walked to the family's garage. The garage's cool interior was a nice respite from the scorching Mississippi heat, but their nostrils again detected the coppery scent of blood, and when they peered inside the Wagners' car, they saw that the front seat of the Chevrolet sedan was streaked with red. Glancing upward, they glimpsed another shocking clue. In the center of the garage was a single lightbulb stained with a bloody handprint. The bulb had no pull chain or light switch with which to turn it on. To turn the lightbulb on, it had to be tightened in its socket and loosened to turn it off. With the evidence pointing toward the death of Mamie Wagner, a black cloud of grief descended on the crime scene.

6
PREACHER VS. BUSINESSMAN

Always hoping to increase his family's financial wealth, D.R. Wagner became part-owner of the Yocona Twine Factory in 1877. With the end of the Civil War twelve years earlier, the South's economy was left in shambles, leading many people to believe that industrialization was the key to rebuilding the South. So, in 1865 a group of Water Valley's most powerful businessmen formed a joint-stock company to bring the Mississippi Central Railroad to town. The railroad meant jobs, and jobs led to recovery. The joint-stock company's first official act was the purchase of a one-mile tract of land in the northern part of town. Hoping to entice the railroad even more, the new company donated a large section of the newly purchased land to the Mississippi Railroad Company while reserving the remainder for an undetermined plant to be built at a future date.

With Reconstruction on the minds of most every Southerner, it took the overworked Mississippi State Legislature two years to approve the company's charter. The charter authorized the new company to establish several businesses, including a factory that would manufacture wool and cotton goods. In 1868, a group of Swedes was brought to Water Valley by Gus Burgland, a stockholder and manager, to work in the factory. Not being acclimated to the South's harsh humidity and heat, the Swedes did not last long; many of them succumbed to heat stroke and dehydration. For the moment, the venture failed, and the factory was converted into a hospital.

In 1877, under the direction of D.R. Wagner, the company, previously the Water Valley Manufacturing Company, was reorganized and renamed Yocona Mills. With his usual work ethic, D.R. rolled up his sleeves and started to get the factory running as soon as possible. Of course, factories aren't viable overnight, especially one that had failed in its infancy, but in April 1881, the *Vicksburg Herald* reported that "the cotton factory at Water Valley, which has been idle for some years, will soon be put in repair and run again." The hard work paid off, and in 1882, the Mississippi State Legislature deemed that any industry in Mississippi that dealt in cotton, yarn, woolen goods, or fabrics would be given tax-free exemptions on all their machinery.

By 1882, the factory was transforming three bales of cotton per day into around seven thousand pounds of twine a week. At first, the factory employed sixty-five employees who were tasked with unbaling the cotton, cleaning it, running the machinery, and transporting the finished product to the railroad. As the company's production increased, so did its profits; the *Southern-Live-Stock-Journal* revealed in April 1891, "The Yokona [*sic*] cotton factory at Water Valley has just declared a quarterly dividend of five percent." Rising from the ashes of failure, under the leadership of

This is a Lewis Hines photograph of the Yocona Twine Factory employees. Hines states in the description of his photo, "The three smallest ones in the front row hang around and help some. The baby doesn't work—yet. The rest are steady workers." *Library of Congress.*

D.R. Wagner, the Yocona Twine Factory quickly became the largest and most profitable twine factory in the United States. Despite its success, there was one major problem with the factory: Many of its employees were children.

Regardless of the dark cloud of child labor hanging over the factory, good fortune continued to shine on Water Valley in 1882 when the Illinois Central Railroad purchased both the Mississippi Central Railroad and the North/South Rail Line, which ran from New Orleans to Chicago. The significance of the rail lines meant that thousands of people traveled through Water Valley weekly, and when the trains stopped to refuel, the passengers had a chance to shop in the stores.

With the death of William, D.R. became the sole proprietor of Wagner & Company, which, along with the twine mill, quickly made him the richest man in town.

Due to his growing fortune, D.R. and his family built a Queen Anne Victorian house on Dupuy Street in 1890. The house was three stories high, with a balcony on the second floor and another on the roof, which provided the family with the best view in town. D.R. and his family didn't just settle for the largest house; they wanted it to be the most lavishly furnished. With that in mind, D.R., his wife, and their children traveled north to shop, bringing back the most expensive furnishings money could buy.

D.R.'s rising wealth was evidence of his good business sense, which led to his election as the president of the Bank of Water Valley. The bank, a state institution chartered by the Mississippi legislature, opened its doors in 1887 with a cash capital of $35,000. The bank brought financial stability to the growing city, providing small business loans to the ever-growing list of the city's entrepreneurs. In a 1909 advertisement in the *City Itemizer*, the bank, which was still under the direction of D.R. Wagner, stated that it had liberal accommodation for loans and ample provisions to keep all deposits safe. W.B. Wagner, D.R.'s nephew, was the president of the Bank of Water Valley at the time of his murder.

Life continued for the better in 1892 when Water Valley built one of the first water and light plants in the South. The installation of electricity in the town was remarkable because the White House had gotten electricity only a year earlier when Benjamin Harrison was president. Irwin "Ike" Hoover, the White House's chief electrician and later its chief usher, said, "The Harrison family were afraid to turn the lights on and off for fear of getting a shock....I would turn on the lights in the halls and the parlors in the evening and they would burn until I returned the next morning to extinguish them."

Water Valley's power and water plants were a blessing for those who found employment within the two new establishments.

By 1900, Water Valley was a beehive of activity with thirty trains passing through its borders daily. Two of those trains were passenger trains, allowing passengers to shop or grab something to eat in town while the trains refueled. The visitors to the town were nice, but the one thousand jobs that the Illinois Central Railroad created made the citizens of Water Valley fond of the railroad. With more people pouring into the town, the town's leaders worked hard to ensure the health of its citizens, and in November 1900, the *Greenville Times* reported on their efforts: "Water Valley through the excellent water and sewer system, is claiming to be the most healthful city in the state, having improved 45 percent." The town seemed to have everything going for it, but unfortunately, sadness and tragedy were looming.

John Luther Jones, a man who would become an American folk hero, was born in southeastern Missouri on March 14, 1864. When Jones was a teenager, his father, Frank Jones, a schoolteacher, decided that the wilderness of Missouri had little to offer, so he moved his family to Casey, Kentucky. During his time in Kentucky, John Luther earned the nickname Casey Jones,

John Luther Jones, better known as Casey Jones, a train conductor who became an American legend. *Water Valley Historical Society*.

which became as recognizable to most Americans as Babe Ruth or Thomas Edison. Growing up, Jones became obsessed with railroads, and at the age of fifteen, he found employment in Columbus, Kentucky, with the Mobile & Ohio Railroad as a telegrapher. Due to his good work ethic and desire to succeed, Jones was quickly promoted to flagman. As a flagman, he had to remain alert, directing and restricting the movements of trains as they came into town. A hard worker, he was soon promoted to train conductor, the position for which he is best known.

After a successful stint as a conductor for the Mobile & Ohio Railroad, Jones was hired in 1891 by the ever-expanding Illinois Central Line, whose headquarters were in Water Valley. When he moved to town, Jones resided in a boardinghouse along Main Street. With little leisure time, he did not participate in many city activities; regardless, he became a well-known citizen of the town. As his reputation as a train conductor grew, it became abundantly clear that he had an aversion to being late and he didn't mind pushing his locomotives to the breaking point to ensure he showed up on time.

On April 20, 1900, Jones pulled into Memphis, Tennessee, from Canton, Mississippi. Tired, sweaty, and looking forward to some sleep, he was told that the conductor scheduled for the return run had fallen ill. Whether he wanted the extra income or wanted to help a friend, we will never know, but Jones volunteered to conduct the return run to Canton. It was a decision that would end his life but make him a legend. In the early morning hours, Casey Jones climbed aboard Engine No. 1 and headed back to Canton.

Due to the confusion about who would replace the sick conductor, the train was already an hour and a half behind schedule. Opening the engine, Jones pushed the train to around one hundred miles per hour. Nearing Vaughan, Mississippi, Sim Webb, the train's fireman, warned Jones that there was a train on the tracks up ahead. Desperate to keep the trains from colliding, Jones applied the brake and began to blow his whistle. In a matter of seconds, it was clear that the trains would collide, so Jones told Webb to jump from the train and save himself. As he hit the ground, Webb could only watch in horror as the two trains collided. The thirty-seven-year-old Casey Jones died when he was struck in the throat by debris. Fortunately, Jones's quick thinking saved all the passengers and crewmen on both trains. Casey's sacrifice has been recorded in songs, poetry, books, and plays. Today, Water Valley has a museum dedicated to the most famous conductor of all time.

As tragic as Casey Jones's death was, there was an incident the year before that sent even bigger shock waves through Water Valley. Having grown up without a father for most of his life, W.B. Wagner looked to his uncle D.R. as a father figure and a person whom he wanted to emulate in the business world. During childhood, W.B. and Andrew Wagner could be seen working in the family clothing store, and when he grew up, W.B. even invested in the Yocona Twine Factory. With two Wagner men at the helm of the factory, its success skyrocketed, but there was one man, Reverend H.P. Gibbs, who could not overlook the factory's use of child labor or the tenement living of the factory's employees.

H.P. Gibbs was born at Bourton-on-the-Hill, Cotswold District, Gloucestershire, England, on July 19, 1865. Records are unclear about how or why the Gibbs family immigrated to the United States but whatever the reason, it led to H.P. Gibbs eventually settling in Water Valley. One of the most important events in Gibbs's life happened on December 18, 1888, when he married Carlotta Hargrove in Lowndes County, Mississippi. Carlotta was the youngest of six children born in Columbus, Mississippi, to William Hargrove. Prior to the Civil War, Hargrove had been a planter who owned nine slaves in 1860. Having been born and raised on a plantation, Carlotta's ideas about labor were possibly different from her English-born husband, but even if they were, she supported him in whatever he pursued.

H.P., who was an ordained Methodist minister, was ecstatic when he received the news that he had been appointed the minister of the North Main Street Methodist Church in Water Valley. Gathering up their possessions, he and Carlotta moved to the boom town, where he quickly got to work. Carlotta was also delighted in her new role as a minister's wife.

As a minister, Reverend Gibbs believed deeply in the second great commandment, found in Mark 12:31, "Thou shalt love thy neighbor as thyself." Known as a man of action, Reverend Gibbs began to crusade for the town's downtrodden and the less fortunate. In his opinion, the town's least fortunate people were those who were employed at the Yocona Twine Factory. Not only did he find child labor deplorable, but he also was angry that many factory workers lived in the tenement housing located east of the factory. With their deplorable wages, many of the workers lived in homes poorly furnished with orange crates and other items they scavenged from the town dump.

Believing that the pen was mightier than the sword, Reverend Gibbs began to write a series of scathing articles about the treatment of the Yocona workers. In one article, he wrote that the Wagners were working their employees at starvation levels. In his last article in the series, he wrote,

"The morals of the people of the factory are too well known for me to enter into details." He believed that the workers' surroundings, their low wages, and their tenement housing were contributing to their moral degradation.

Of course, D.R. and W.B. Wagner vehemently disagreed, asserting that the articles were libel and that Reverend Gibbs should be held responsible for his actions. In 1899, the *Sentinel*, a Grenada, Mississippi newspaper, reported that an argument to dismiss a bill of injunction in the case of Wagner, et al., representing the Yocona Mills at Water Valley, Mississippi, versus Revs. H.P. Gibbs, H.C. Moorehead et al., was heard by Chancellor J.C. Longstreet in Grenada. According to the article, the case became famous, because, at the time, Mississippi had a constitutional provision protecting ministers who were attempting to help the poor. Reverend Gibbs's case was pushing the provision to the max, and most of the state was waiting to see whether the state would rule in favor of religion or business. If the courts had ruled sooner, Water Valley might have avoided a horrible and controversial event.

On April 1, with his last article having been published and circulated just days before, Reverend Gibbs was confined to bed with a high fever from an unknown illness. The reverend was so ill that he remained in bed on Sunday. On Monday, April 3, Reverend Gibbs, feeling better, rode his buggy into town to pay bills. Stopping in front of Quinn & Goodwin's Hardware Store, Reverend Gibbs was shocked when D.R. Wagner rushed forward to confront him about his series of articles. His anger having reached its boiling point, D.R. slapped Reverend Gibbs twice across the face. Stunned, Reverend Gibbs sat, mouth agape, while John Wagner, D.R.'s son, and W.B. Wagner confronted him, asking, "Will you write any more articles about Yocona anymore?" Gibbs replied that he would continue to write the articles if the injustices in the factory continued. Enraged, W.B. balled up his fist and hit the reverend in the face. Still not satisfied, W.B. grabbed Gibbs by the throat and began to choke him. Turning the other cheek, Reverend Gibbs offered no resistance, other than trying to pull W.B.'s hands away from his throat. Fortunately, before the incident turned fatal, W.B. released the reverend and walked quickly down the street.

Returning home, Reverend Gibbs returned to his sickbed, and twenty-two days after the attack, on April 23, he passed away. The attack and death of the prominent minister created a journalistic field day. Almost every newspaper in the region printed what they believed to be the correct account of the reverend's death. The *Sentinel* reported, "His [Gibbs] purpose was to ameliorate the condition of employees and to mitigate the hardships to which they were exposed. For this expression of human feeling, he was assaulted in broad daylight and on the busiest street in the city. He made no resistance, and it surmised that from the effects of the assault and his deep humiliation, he contracted the illness to his death." On May 19, the *Commonwealth*, a newspaper printed in Greenwood, Mississippi, attempted to discredit an earlier article published in the *West Point Times*, when it reported, "The article shows what misinformation leads to. This article [referring to the *West Point* article] was written without possessing all the facts in the case. In the first place, the physicians say that Reverend Gibbs's death was not a result of the blows that he received at the hands of Mr. Wagner; again, he was not just up from a sick bed or was not horsewhipped by Mr. Wagner or his nephew, but was struck by the latter with his fist and instead of dying the next day, was down on the street and did not die until twenty days later from complications of other diseases." With so many reports muddying the waters, people drew their own conclusions, but Carlotta Gibbs wanted the courts to decide whether the Wagners should be held responsible for her husband's death.

Carlotta Gibbs had been a model minister's wife, and despite her husband's death, she never blamed God for her misfortunes. However, that did not stop her praying for the swift hand of justice to come down on the Wagner family. Hoping for a big payday, many of the area's most prominent lawyers rushed to aid Carlotta in filing a wrongful death suit for $50,000 against the Wagner family. With personal wealth of $200,000, D.R.'s family circled the wagons, hiring a team of lawyers to defend themselves against the angry widow. As with many civil cases, *Daniel R. Wagner v. Carlotta H. Gibbs* would not be settled quickly. Almost three years passed before the Mississippi Supreme Court ruled in favor of Gibbs, awarding her $2,000 for the assault and battery committed by D.R. and W.B. Wagner. No other charges were brought against them, and eventually, the dust settled surrounding Reverend Gibbs's death, but trouble for the Yocona Twine Factory was far from over.

7
FINDING MAMIE WAGNER

A strange quiet fell over Water Valley, as many of the stores in the town remained closed as a sign of respect for the dead banker and his missing wife. As soon as Sheriff Doyle, Marshal Redwine, and the other investigators exited the Wagners' garage, one of the volunteers who had been searching for Mamie ran up and shouted, "We found her!"

"Alive?" Sheriff Doyle asked, despite knowing the answer.

The volunteer cast his eyes toward the ground and said, "No sir, she is dead."

"Show us the way," Sheriff Doyle commanded.

Jumping into Sheriff Doyle's car, Detective Fox and Sheriff Doyle carefully made their way through the growing crowd surrounding the Wagner home. By the time they turned on the small country road where the body had been found, a crowd of onlookers had gathered and were staring down the embankment at the corpse of Mamie Wagner. Pushing the crowd back, Sheriff Doyle ordered that the ground be searched as far as thirty to forty yards around the victim. As with any murder case, every piece of evidence, no matter how small, could be crucial in breaking the case and bringing a killer or killers to justice. The search resulted only in the discovery of two sets of male footprints, which Sheriff Doyle was convinced were the same size as the ones found at the Wagners' home.

When Detective Fox and Sheriff Doyle finally descended the steep bank, the scene was more brutal than they could have imagined. Later, in *Master Detective* magazine, Detective Fox wrote, "I have encountered many shocking

A crowd of onlookers at the top of the bank where the body of Mamie Wagner was lying. The arrow points to where they located her body. *The Master Detective magazine*.

scenes during my career as a detective, but I hope it will never again fall my lot to view a scene similar to that which awaited us at the foot of that roadside cliff where our gaze fell upon the terrible spectacle of the slain banker's wife, the ghastly victim of inhuman brutality."

Ms. Wagner was lying on her side, clothes disheveled and soaked with blood. For Sheriff Doyle, who had known her well, it was a strange contrast to the usually meticulously dressed Mamie. Like her husband, her head was severely lacerated by what the investigators assumed was the axe found in her dining room. Her most gruesome injury was that her neck had been slashed multiple times, causing her blood to pour out onto the sandy ground of the embankment.

After collecting every possible piece of evidence, Sheriff Doyle left the difficult task of carrying Mamie Wagner's body up the embankment to his deputies and the county coroner. Sliding into the front seat of a police cruiser, Sheriff Doyle and Detective Fox were silent as they drove the two miles back to Wagner Street.

Marshal Redwine, hands shoved deep into his pockets, met them at the curb and asked, "Well…how was it?"

"Horrible," Sheriff Doyle said. "Did you question the neighbors?"

Redwine nodded. "None of them saw a thing."

Sucking air between his teeth, Sheriff Doyle said, "Well let's go see what the medical examiner has to say."

Loading back into their cars, they headed downtown to where the bodies of Mamie and W.B. were held. As they stepped from the car, a gust of wind picked up and Sheriff Doyle clamped one of his large, calloused hands to his hat to keep it from blowing away. One of the lawmen removed a pack of Lucky Strikes from his pocket and passed them around. The lawmen stood smoking while they gave the medical examiner time to clean up the bodies.

"You gentlemen ready?" Sheriff Doyle asked when he deemed enough time had gone by.

Leading the way, Marshal Redwine climbed the stairs, opened the door, and stepped inside. The smell of death mixed with alcohol flooded their nostrils, causing some of the investigators' stomachs to churn. The medical examiner, a local doctor, was standing by the metal tables staring down at the two brutalized bodies. Both bodies looked as if they had been at war, and in a way, they had—they fought for their lives and lost.

Mamie's face, clean now from the sand that covered it earlier, was more bruised and lacerated than the lawmen had assumed. The medical examiner determined W.B. had died from blunt force trauma. Mamie's cause of death was listed as blood loss due to her throat being slit three times.

"What was their time of death?" Marshal Redwine asked.

Removing his wire-rimmed glasses, the medical examiner rubbed the bridge of his nose and said, "Between 8:00 p.m. and 12:00 a.m. last night. Both were still in their clothes, indicating that they never made it to bed last night."

With the cause of death revealed, the investigators set about trying to establish a motive for the murders. With W.B. and Mamie being the richest couple in town, robbery was at the forefront of the investigators' minds. There was only one problem: Nothing was missing from the Wagner home, and when they found W.B.'s body, he was still wearing an expensive ring. Had the killers broken into the Wagner home hoping to force W.B., the president of the Bank of Water Valley, to unlock the bank vault so that it could be looted? If so, had W.B. refused, and in their rage, they murdered the couple? The investigators all agreed that neither motive seemed likely. The viciousness of the attacks pointed to something personal, something driven by anger.

With no clear motive, Sheriff Doyle knew that only good police work would bring the murderers to justice. That is why he was pleased to see Sheriff Fred Nason, a fingerprint expert from Grenada County, arrive and volunteer to help gather evidence.

A lifelong resident of Grenada County, Fred Nason was born in May 1894 to Robert and Ida Nason. Robert Nason worked hard plowing, planting, and praying for a good harvest from the Mississippi soil. His family, like thousands of others in the Magnolia State, lived hand to mouth. Despite their poverty, Fred and Ida raised their children to be grateful for what little they had. They also raised their children to be patriotic, which was evident when their son Fred volunteered to fight in World War I.

It was June 28, 1914, and Sarajevo was bubbling with excitement as Archduke Franz Ferdinand and his wife Sophie's motorcade drove at a breakneck pace toward Sarajevo's city hall for an event where the archduke would serve as the guest of honor. In their hurry to get there, three drivers changed history by accidentally turning down the wrong street. Unfortunately, a disgruntled nineteen-year-old man named Gavrilo Princip was waiting to strike. A member of the Black Hand, a secret Serbian society fighting for Serbian independence, Princip pulled a revolver and fired two shots, striking the archduke in the throat and Sophie in the abdomen. During his interrogation, Gavrilo Princip said he had never meant to hurt Sophie.

Before help arrived, both Sophie and the archduke succumbed to their injuries. With the heir to the throne dead, Austria-Hungary declared war on Serbia, beginning the War to End All Wars—World War I. With many European countries having united under the alliance system, Russia rushed to the aid of Serbia while Germany aligned itself with Austria-Hungary. On the other side of the Atlantic, Americans waited with bated breath hoping that they would not be drawn into this global conflict.

An isolationist country, the United States wanted to stay as far away from the war as possible; however, Germany seemed to have other plans. On May 7, 1915, the *Lusitania*, a British-owned luxury steamship, was torpedoed by a German U-boat, killing 1,195 people, including 128 Americans. The death of the 128 Americans strained the relationship between America and Germany to the breaking point; the United States decided it was better to take the loss than enter a war that might lead to hundreds of thousands of American deaths.

As disturbing as the sinking of the *Lusitania* was, Germany's next action against the United States seemed even more surreal. With German U-boats destroying American merchant ships that were trying to reach England, Germany was not honoring the Sussex Pledge, an agreement to refrain from sinking unidentified merchant ships in the North Atlantic. With Germany not honoring its pledge, the United States withdrew diplomatic relations from Germany. In retaliation, German Foreign Minister to Mexico Arthur Zimmermann sent a telegram to the Mexican government asking them to attack the United States in a joint effort with Germany. Fortunately, British intelligence intercepted, deciphered, and sent the telegram to the United States, further fanning the flames of war.

With Germany's unrelenting submarine warfare on American merchant ships, the United States finally had enough, and on April 6, 1917, Congress declared war on Germany. With a small peacetime army, America needed soldiers quickly, so 2.8 million men were drafted to fight the dreaded Huns. Other American men, fired by patriotic passion, rushed to volunteer for an all-expense-paid chance to fight for democracy. Fred Nason was one of those men.

On leave from basic training, Fred was interviewed by the *Grenada Sentinel* about his decision to volunteer. "I wanted to do my part toward establishing a democratic government in all countries," he said. Shortly after the interview, he was sent to Hoboken, New Jersey, and then he was shipped to Europe on August 31, 1918. By the time he arrived in Europe, the war would go on for only four more months before Germany signed an armistice on November 11, 1918. Despite the war being over, Fred didn't return from France until May 22, 1919.

Like millions of other veterans, Fred returned home a changed man. Hoping to find a career he loved, he ran for and won the position of Grenada county tax collector. Tiring of his revenue position, Fred ran for sheriff of Grenada County and won in a landslide. At the time of W.B. and Mamie's murders, Sheriff Nason was thirty-six years old, single, and living as a boarder in the house of Graham and Blanche Clark.

With few fingerprint experts in the state of Mississippi, Sheriff Nason was a welcome addition to the investigation, and he and Captain Wattam were quickly put to work examining and filing each fingerprint at the murder scene. At the time of the murders, fingerprinting had been accepted as a reliable form of evidence by law enforcement all over the world. Developed in 1894 by Sir Edward Henry, fingerprinting categorizes four types of fingertip impressions: loops, whirls, composites, and arches. The National Forensic Science Technology Center stated, "No two people have ever been found to have the same fingerprints—including identical twins."

Unfortunately for Nason and Wattam, there was not a large collection of fingerprints at the sheriff's office. More than likely, Sheriff Doyle and Marshal Redwine would have no choice but to turn to the tried-and-true method of interrogating suspects.

8
CHILD LABOR AND THE YOCONA TWINE FACTORY

As the nineteenth century ended, America emerged as the world's leading industrialized nation, producing more goods than its citizens could consume. Unfortunately, the rich were getting richer, and the poor were getting poorer, and the government was doing very little to protect the average American. As poverty increased, every member of a family—man, woman, and child—was forced to work. By 1910, an unbelievable two million children were slaving away in coal mines, factories, textile mills, canning factories, and other labor-intensive jobs.

Regardless of how hard they worked, children were always paid less than other workers. Another benefit of employing the young was that their hands were tiny enough to handle small tools, and they could reach tight places where adult hands would not fit. Unfortunately, the childhood of child laborers was nonexistent as they worked six days a week, eight to twelve hours a day. The hatred for child labor helped unify people across the nation and led to the formation of the National Child Labor Committee (NCLC).

It was April 1904 when the NCLC held its first meeting in New York City's Carnegie Hall. Its first order of business was to appoint Felix Adler as the organization's first chairman. With an urgent need to end child labor, the organization attracted prominent reformers such as Florence Kelley, Jane Addams, Grover Cleveland, and others. Gaining traction, the NCLC received a national charter from Congress in 1907. The charter legitimized their efforts nationally. As influential as many of the members were, there was one man, Lewis Hine, a photographer, whose images would bring trouble to the doorstep of the Yocona Twine Factory and the Wagner family.

Born on September 26, 1874, in Oshkosh, Wisconsin, Lewis Hine was forced to grow up quickly when his father was killed in a tragic accident when Lewis was just a child. Determined to attend college, Hine joined the labor force early to raise money for his future. Captivated by societal problems, he enrolled at the University of Chicago, where he majored in sociology. Hine also attended the prestigious Columbia University and New York University before being hired as a teacher at the Ethical Cultural School in New York City. As a teacher, Hine encouraged his students to use photography to capture historical and social events. During a field trip with his sociology class, Hine and his students photographed immigrants as they stepped foot on American soil for the first time. The more pictures he took, the more convinced he became that he could use photography to enact societal change.

In 1909, Hine published his most influential works, *Child Labour in the Carolinas* and *Day Laborers Before Their Time*. The photo collections included children, some as young as eight, working in coal mines and textile factories scattered throughout the Carolinas. Through his camera lens, he peeled back the layers of child labor, exposing the dangerous working conditions and tenement living. In 1911, his work garnered the attention of the NCLC, which hired him to travel throughout the eastern United States to photograph child labor practices.

To gain access to factories, Hine often posed as a postcard vendor, insurance salesman, industrial photographer, Bible salesman, or anything else that would allow him access inside a factory. Hiding a notebook in his pocket, he would furiously scribble down the names, ages, and other relevant information from the children he cautiously interviewed before the factory owners caught on to his real motive. He also used the buttons on his jacket to guess how tall the children he interviewed were. As his reputation grew, he was often refused entrance to factories by angry owners, who occasionally called the police to intervene on their behalf. When denied entry to a factory, he would wait outside for the children to exit the workplace, hoping to take their photograph. If given permission, he would follow them home to interview their parents and photograph their poor living conditions.

In May 1911, Lewis Hine, camera in hand, traveled to Water Valley, Mississippi, to investigate the conditions of the Yocona Twine Factory. With the Mississippi heat soaring and the factory having little or no ventilation, he found the workers slaving away in intolerable and unsafe conditions. How much he was able to investigate the factory is unknown; however, he took a group photo of the factory's employees posing behind the factory. Almost half of the workers were children, some of them as young as eight. Hine labeled the photograph: "Nearly the entire force, Yoona (i.e. Yocona) Mills, Water Valley, Miss. Some of the smallest workers are not in the photo. The three smallest ones in the front row hang around to help some. Baby doesn't work, yet. The rest are steady workers. (See Hine's report for data about the past earnings of this mill). Location: Water Valley, Mississippi." While in Water Valley, Hine also took pictures of the tenement living where many of the factory's employees lived.

With the factory receiving negative publicity, D.R. and W.B. Wagner must have been livid. However, Lewis Hine and the NCLC were too far out of reach for even the Wagner family to touch. Sadly, Hine's hard work didn't pay off immediately. The Yocona factory continued employing children for years after Hine photographed its workers.

The Yocona Twine Factory's bad publicity faded quickly into the background as Water Valley gained national attention when the Illinois

The shorter boy on the right is Dorris Fabanks; he had been working in the Yocona Twine Factory for a year. His brother to the left had been working at the factory for six years. *Library of Congress.*

Central Railroad's Shopmen's Labor Union went on strike. The union consisted of machinists, blacksmiths, engineers, boilermakers, electricians, and sheet metal workers. Responsible for repairing, constructing, and maintaining all the rail cars on the ICR, these workers were indispensable for the railroad's success. With such heavy responsibility weighing on them, the union members demanded more than just the bare minimum from their employers.

Early in 1911, the railroad's managers sat down with union representatives and agreed to several of the union's demands. Despite the negotiations having gone well, railroad management was angry about bending to the union's demands. On the other hand, with the taste of victory fresh on its tongue, the union forced the ICR management to return to the negotiation table in June 1911. This time, railroad management refused to give in to the union's demands, and thirty thousand workers in twenty-four cities left their jobs and walked straight to the picket lines. At first, the strike was peaceable, but it would soon turn violent.

The first round of violence erupted in McComb, Mississippi, on October 3, 1911, when union members rushed train cars loaded with 450 strikebreakers. ICR management had hired African American strikebreakers as a tactic to inflame the Southern union members. The strategy worked, as union members armed with bricks and guns began firing at the strikebreakers, who fired back. Unbelievably, during the conflict, around one thousand shots were exchanged, but only one man, a union member and well-known citizen of McComb, was seriously injured after being hit in the head with a brick. Fearing more violence, Sheriff Holmes of Pike County deputized armed citizens to patrol the streets of McComb until state troops could be deployed to the city. At the request of the sheriff, Mississippi Governor Edmond Favor Noel, worried that more violence would erupt, deployed three companies of the state military to McComb to prevent further bloodshed.

Born in Holmes County on March 4, 1856, Edmond Noel would eventually be educated in Louisville, Kentucky, where he studied law. After graduation, he established his first practice in Lexington, Mississippi. For Noel, practicing law was an easy transition into politics, and he was able to win seats in both the Mississippi Senate and the Mississippi House of Representatives before being elected governor on August 22, 1907. During his years in office, he was a progressive governor, especially where education was concerned. Despite their liking for Governor Noel, many

Mississippians were angry that he sent troops to McComb. Noel's plan worked, and the troops ended the violence in McComb, but the violence was far from over.

As Water Valley was the Illinois Central Railroad headquarters, tensions in town ran high, reaching a fever pitch on the night of October 6, when over one hundred shots were fired between union members and strikebreakers. Once again, Governor Noel responded quickly, dispatching state troops to Water Valley to protect the railroad. In an issue of the *Columbus Commercial* on October 12, 1911, Captain W.S. Mullins, commander of the Columbus Rifles, reported that things had been quiet in Water Valley. He also stated that the troops were being comfortably quartered, were fed well, and were well prepared for any violence that might arise. Despite the troops' good living conditions, some of the men from the Caledonia Rifle Company had failed to report for duty toward the end of October. An article in the *Columbus Commercial* warned the AWOL members of the Caledonia Rifles would face a court-martial if they did not report to Water Valley as soon as possible. The article was clear: Governor Noel intended to keep the troops there until the threat of violence was over.

On January 17, 1912, despite the best efforts of Governor Noel, violence in McComb broke out again; this time, five Black strikebreakers were shot. Three of the strikebreakers died due to their injuries. Later that year, the violence reached as far as Mojave, California, when a railcar inspector named Ed Lefevre was shot and killed by an unknown assailant. Investigators never caught who killed Lefevre, but they were convinced that his death had been a result of the strike.

With Water Valley and McComb embroiled in violence, the ICR relocated the city's mechanic shop to Jackson. Tired of violence, loss of work, and loss of money, the ICR finally agreed to the union's demands, restoring peace to McComb and Water Valley. Hoping to make up for lost time and lost pay, workers in both towns got back to work as quickly as they could.

9

LET THE INTERROGATIONS BEGIN

Having gathered evidence and inspected the bodies, Sheriff Doyle returned with Detective Fox to the sheriff's office to begin interrogating witnesses and possible suspects. At the office, Doyle and Fox were met by a large crowd of lawmen, including Undersheriff A.K. Burt, Sheriff Doyle's son Deputy C.T. Doyle Jr., Captain Wattam, Sheriff Nason, and others, eager to solve the murders. Stepping into his office, Sheriff Doyle removed his hat and ran his hand through his sweaty, matted hair. He felt like he had aged a decade since entering the Wagner home just hours before.

Glancing around at the anxious faces, Sheriff Doyle commanded, "Bring in everybody who might be connected with these murders and do it fast."

Several deputies, who had been standing around, scattered like a covey of quail as they rushed out the door to round up suspects. Satisfied that his orders had been followed, Sheriff Doyle went into the interrogation room, sat down, and waited for Callie Wiggins to be brought in to be questioned.

The African American cook and housekeeper was wide-eyed as she shuffled into the small room.

"Afternoon," Sheriff Doyle said. "Thank you for coming in to talk with us."

Callie nodded, her eyes trained on the floor.

Reaching into his shirt pocket, Detective Fox pulled out a pack of Lucky Strikes and slapped them against the palm of his hand. Peeling the foil from the pack, he shook out a cigarette, removed it, and clamped it firmly between his teeth. As he ran a match across the tabletop, a flame blazed to life, and he held it up to the cigarette. The end of the cigarette glowed red, and he inhaled and then blew out a cloud of smoke toward the ceiling. He held the pack out to Callie, who glanced up briefly and shook her head.

"Do you know anyone who might have borne a grudge against your employers?" Sheriff Doyle asked.

Callie said, "No suh, I sho' don't."

After questioning her at length, Detective Fox and Sheriff Doyle were convinced that she had nothing to do with the murders.

"Well…we feel like you told as much as you can," Sheriff Doyle said, placing his hands on the table and pushing himself up from his seat.

Daring a glance, Callie looked up and said, "I did see Sam Whitaker there this morning."

Sitting back down, Sheriff Doyle glanced at Detective Fox and said, "Sam Whitaker, huh?"

Most people who knew W.B. and Mamie Wagner knew that their houseboy was Sam Whitaker, a small, dark-skinned young man who looked more like he was thirteen than eighteen. A wistful smile always seemed to dance on his lips, even during the most serious moments.

"What was he doing there so early?" Sheriff Doyle asked.

With another look at Sheriff Doyle, Callie replied, "Jaybirds been picking Mr. Wagner's cherries and Sam brought a slingshot to rid the orchard of pests."

"Oh…I see," Sheriff Doyle said, raising his eyebrows. With the body of W.B. Wagner found next to the cherry orchard, had Sam been the one to dig the shallow grave for his employer? "Did Sam say anything to you?"

"Yas-sah, I b'lieve he did," Callie said.

Callie continued, "He told me, the white folks ain't there…an th' ain't no use fo' you to go in th' house, Callie, was what he said."

With this revelation, a light went off in Sheriff Doyle's head. Why would Sam have said that W.B. and Mamie were gone? Had he knocked on their door? Was it possible that Sam, a quiet, unassuming young man, had murdered his employers?

"I guess that's about it," Sheriff Doyle said, rising to his feet.

By the time Sheriff Doyle was done interviewing Callie Wiggins, his deputies had brought in five possible suspects, but the sheriff had only one man in mind: Sam Whitaker.

"Someone…bring me Sam Whitaker, now!" Sheriff Doyle commanded.

It wasn't long before Sam Whitaker, a deputy on each side of him, shuffled inside the sheriff's office. He wore a devil-may-care expression as he walked inside and plopped down at the interrogation table.

Crushing a cigarette in the ashtray at the center of the table, Detective Fox leaned forward and took stock of the young man sitting across from him.

"What do you know about these murders?" Sheriff Doyle asked.

Shrugging, Sam said, "Nuthin."

"Where were you last night?"

"Home," answered Sam.

After about an hour of questioning, Sam had not given up anything. Usually an astute judge of character, Detective Fox had studied the young Black man the whole time he was questioned but was unable to tell if he was innocent or guilty.

Glancing down, Detective Fox noticed that Sam's shoe had a stain that looked suspiciously like blood. Leaning over, Detective Fox whispered something to Undersheriff Burt, whose gaze immediately fell on Sam's shoes.

"How did you get blood on your shoes?" Burt asked, pointing his finger at the shoe in question.

Glancing down, unperturbed, Sam said, "Don't know suh, less'n I stepped in it somewhere."

Reaching across the table, Detective Fox grabbed Sam by the arm and inspected his fingernails. Specks of a red substance, possibly blood, covered his unkempt nails. The two lawmen glanced at each other, believing they had their man.

When Captain Wattam and Sheriff Nason returned from dusting the crime scene for prints, they laid out their equipment, an ink pad, and fingerprint cards. Under orders from the sheriff, they fingerprinted Sam Whitaker. After the prints dried, Wattam and Nason began to compare the fingerprints against those found at the crime scene. While they were busy looking through their magnifying glasses, other officers took prints of Sam's shoes and began to compare those to the ones found on the bloody floor of the Wagners' bedroom.

When they finished, a deputy escorted Sam back into the interrogation room, where the young man became cold and distant. After a short time, Sheriff Nason poked his head in the door and motioned for Sheriff Doyle to follow him into the other room.

Detective Fox watched the men speak in hushed whispers before Sheriff Doyle reentered the room. The sheriff said, "Sam, looks like we have a problem. Your fingerprints matched the bloody ones found on the lightbulb at the Wagner's garage. So…the question is, why did you do it?"

Sam's smile gave way to a frown as he finally grasped the gravity of his situation, and without the counsel of a lawyer, Sam said, "Mr. Wagner slapped me Monday for stealing his gun. He told me that he was going to whip me th' next day. I took his axe an' went in the house last night…" Sam paused, either afraid to continue or too stunned to recount the night's horrors.

The room fell silent at the admitted brutality of this small, seemingly harmless young man.

From left to right: Sam Whitaker, Adele Whitaker, and Deputy Leon Ware. *The Master Detective magazine*.

"And then what? Go on," Sheriff Doyle said.

Clearing his throat, Sam continued. "I found Mrs. Wagner in the dining room, and I struck her over the head! She fell across the dining table. I heard someone coming and I ran to the back door, leaving Mrs. Wagner on th' floor in her room.…It was Mr. Wagner at th' back porch. I hit him on th' head with th' axe! He fell dead!"

The confession seemed to pour out of Sam: "Emmett Shaw was waiting for me in the yard. He helped me carry Mr. Wagner out and we found a shovel in the garage. We buried him in a shallow grave, cause we didn't have much time."

It wasn't Sheriff Doyle's first time hearing a murderer confess, but the malice in Sam's voice and the brutality of the crime made his stomach churn. Despite Mamie and W.B.'s reputation as being cantankerous and demanding, no one deserved to die like they had.

Motioning for one of his deputies to come forward, Sheriff Doyle said, "Go find Emmett Shaw and bring him here. Quick as you can."

Emmett Shaw, a thirty-five-year-old Black man and former porter at the Wagner Clothing Store, was born in 1887 in Lincoln County, Mississippi. He was raised by his uncle Tom Armstrong, a sharecropper whose large house included his children, nieces, nephews, and other family members. As sharecroppers, they spent much time trying to scratch out a meager living from the Mississippi soil. As Emmett grew, he quickly found few opportunities outside of farming and domestic work for men and women of color in Mississippi. When World War I broke out, despite the limited opportunities for Black Americans, Emmett and millions of other Black men were expected to sign up for the Selective Service, which would allow them to be drafted into military service. Shortly after signing up, Emmett was drafted and placed into Company D Reserve Labor Company at Columbia, Mississippi, on August 31, 1918. Never having left the United States during his service, Emmett was honorably discharged from the military on February 15, 1919.

Returning to Mississippi, Emmett, twenty-five, settled into Water Valley and married Lena, who was fourteen at the time of their wedding. Two years later, Lena gave birth to their first child. She would go on to have four more of Emmett's children before he was involved in the Wagner murders in 1931. With five children to feed, Emmett desperately needed a job and considered himself lucky when he was hired as a porter at the Wagner & Company Clothing Store.

At the time of the murders, Emmett was not employed by the Wagner Company, having been fired for petty theft shortly before May 5. Convicted by a local judge, Emmett had been sentenced to serve on a chain gang, which he had been doing just hours before Sam Whitaker killed W.B. and Mamie Wagner.

Unfortunately for Emmett, due to the pettiness of his crime and the fact that he was well-behaved, he was given the position as a jail trustee. As a trustee, he returned home every night to his wife and children after laboring all day for the town. His position as a trustee served as his downfall. If he had been incarcerated on the night of the murders, he would not have been able to cover up the Wagners' deaths. He also would have had an airtight alibi.

While the manhunt continued for Emmett Shaw, Sam Whitaker continued to give details about the murders.

"Tell us what happened next," Sheriff Doyle said.

Taking on a more somber tone, Sam said, "My sister, Adele Whitaker, came up while me an' Emmett wuz burying Mr. Wagner, an' we made her help us. I then went back to th' room where Missus Mamie was groaning on th' floor. We picked her up and carried her to th' garage. I turned on th' light so's we could see how to put her into her auto."

Detective Fox asked, "Who drove the car?"

"I did," Sam said, "and when we got to th' cliff about three miles away an' hurled her over it. I looked down and saw that she wasn't dead. I could hear her groaning, so I climbed down to where she was and slashed her throat to put her out of misery."

The coldness of Sam's confession shocked even the most hardened lawmen. Motioning for Sam to get up, Sheriff Doyle escorted the murderer down the hall to a holding cell. Without a lawyer, Sam's eagerness to talk had sealed his fate. There was only one thing left to do: find Emmett to see if his story matched Sam's.

10

THE DEATH OF THE PATRIARCH

In 1914, much to the excitement of the citizens of Water Valley, the Illinois Central Railroad decided to continue to use the town as the main location for the company's train car repair shops. With the railroad strike over, the Wagner family was looking forward to continuing to build their financial success. When 1915 dawned, D.R. Wagner had amassed a personal fortune of just over $800,000, which today would have the purchasing power of $24 million. Unfortunately for D.R., all the money in his bank account couldn't buy good health, and his was deteriorating quickly. He had only one place in mind where he could go: Hot Springs, Arkansas.

Before white men set foot in North America, Native Americans had been taking advantage of the thermal spring in Hot Springs for centuries. The various Native Americans who inhabited the region called the area the "Valley of the Vapors." The area was deemed a neutral location by competing tribes so that their sick members could coalesce in what they believed were healing waters. It wasn't until 1541 that the first Europeans visited the area when Hernando de Soto and his exploration stumbled across the heated springs. De Soto and his crew spent eleven months exploring Arkansas until his death on May 31, 1542.

With Thomas Jefferson acquiring the Louisiana Purchase for $15 million in 1803, the size of the United States doubled, and the concept of Manifest Destiny was born. In 1832, under an executive order from President Andrew Jackson, the hot springs became America's first federal reservation. As the

Water Valley in the summer of 1900. You can see the initials of the Illinois Central Railroad on the engine. *Photo by J.E. France.*

population of Arkansas grew, the reputation of the hot springs as a healing place spread throughout the United States.

In the late 1800s, people from all over the world traveled to soak in the healing waters of Hot Springs, and Victorian bathhouses sprang up like toadstools along the main street. On June 10, 1915, the *City Itemizer* reported, "Mr. D.R. Wagner left last Thursday for Hot Springs, Arkansas, where he will spend a month on account of his health. Hope he will soon return thoroughly restored."

During his stay in Hot Springs, D.R. sought consultation with a specialist to help control his rheumatoid arthritis. The seventy-five-year-old mogul's gnarled and twisted hands had been a source of pain for many years, and he soaked in the hot springs daily. Unfortunately, D.R. never returned to Water Valley, dying from hypostatic pneumonia at two o'clock in the afternoon on July 15, 1915. After Water Valley received the news of D.R.'s death, a black cloud fell over the city. Seven days after his death, the *City Itemizer* ran an article about D.R.'s death stating, "The city of Water Valley has lost one of her most valuable citizens, a man who conservative characteristics made him a preserver and a conserver." Regardless of D.R.'s former struggles with Reverend Gibbs, the people of Water Valley considered him a kind man who would be greatly missed.

D.R.'s funeral service was held at the First Presbyterian Church of Water Valley, where it was standing room only as Reverend J.D. Leslie, D.R.'s former preacher, who had moved to Texas years before, stepped to the pulpit and began to regale the crowd with memories of D.R. mixed with a strong dose of scripture. At the end of his sermon, Reverend Leslie took a seat while the church pianist played a hymn. When the last note rang out, the current minister at the First Presbyterian Church, J.E. Hobson, stepped to the pulpit and stared down at the congregation, many of whom were his current parishioners. Unlike Reverend Leslie, Reverend Hobson had known D.R. during his golden years, which he focused on throughout his eulogy. When the service was over, six pallbearers rose, walked forward, lifted the casket, and carried it outside, placing it into the hearse that would provide D.R. Wagner with his last ride to his eternal resting place. Following the procession, the Wagner family arrived at Oak Hill Cemetery to watch as D.R.'s coffin was lowered slowly into the ground.

Upon D.R.'s death, W.B. became not only the paterfamilias of the Wagner family but also the most powerful man in Water Valley. Unlike D.R., W.B. was often considered ill-tempered and inconsiderate of people's feelings. Despite his attitude differing from his uncle's, his business acumen was just as sharp, and by 1916, he was the president of the Bank of Water Valley, president of Yocona Twine Factory, and president of Wagner & Company Clothing Store, and he had also been elected as the trustee of Water Valley Public Schools.

Regardless of W.B.'s many responsibilities, Wagner & Company Clothing Store held a special place in his heart, and he continued to occupy a hands-on role in the daily operations of the business. In January 1919, he traveled to New York City and Chicago, where he bought an extensive line of spring coats, suits, lace, shirtwaists, and other garments. After his trip, the *North Mississippi Herald* reported that his trip would make Wagner & Co. the most exclusive store in Water Valley, possibly the region. The store's clientele ranged from Water Valley's wealthiest citizens to those who were middle class. The store not only provided a wide range of clothing but also employed Black porters who would deliver to a customer's front door.

Hoping to provide their child with a superior education that only money could buy, W.B. and Mamie enrolled their son, William, in Castle Heights Military School in Lebanon, Tennessee. The academy was founded in 1902 by David Mitchell, president of Cumberland University; A.W. Hooke; and Laban Rice. The initial goal of the academy was to provide quality education for the children, boys and girls alike, of the more affluent families of the

South. However, as World War I took center stage, the academy became a military school and changed its name to Castle Heights Military School. With girls no longer allowed at the academy, their pedagogical practices changed to educate young men in academics, discipline, military knowledge, and calisthenics. As a young man of privilege, William spent his summer vacations traveling to locations that most people from the South, during this time, could only dream of. The *North Mississippi Herald* reported, "Young William Wagner and Cousin John Henry Wagner spent their summer break with the Megunticook Campers in the forest of Maine. Both young men had a very good time and are well-rested for the upcoming school year."

Whether poor or rich, the life of the white people of Water Valley was much different from that of its Black citizens, as evidenced by one of the most infamous events in the city's history. On this day in 1921, it was a mild sixty-five degrees when Angie Cofer rose from her bed, completed some chores around her house, and then decided to visit a relative who lived less than a mile from her home. With the weather being so beautiful, Cofer walked to her relative's home so that she could soak up the beauty of God's creation. When she arrived, they decided that the day was so nice they would stay on the front porch swapping recipes, catching up on local news from the community, and reminiscing about days gone by.

Feeling that she had worn out her welcome, Cofer thanked her relatives for their hospitality, bid them goodbye, and began the short walk home. About a half mile from her house, a Black man rushed from the woods and grabbed her by the arm. Resolved to not go down without a fight, Cofer pulled a knife from her apron and attempted to cut and stab her attacker. The attacker, feeling as if he had bitten off more than he could chew, scrambled away into the woods. With her home empty, Cofer, adrenaline coursing through her veins, rushed back to her relatives' house to report the attack.

After they calmed her down, Cofer's relatives contacted her son, Claude Cofer, who was shocked and blinded by anger. A law-abiding man, Claude Cofer picked up the phone and called the Yalobusha County Sheriff's Office. After speaking with Claude Cofer, Sheriff W.N. Frost immediately dispatched deputies to the scene and to Angie Cofer's relatives' home. When questioned by the police, Cofer could not identify her attacker. Searching the area, the police found no evidence of the attack, so Sheriff Frost contacted a bloodhound handler. Unfortunately, the bloodhounds couldn't make it until two o'clock the next afternoon.

At two o'clock the next day, the handlers met the sheriff at the location of the attack and released the bloodhounds, which crashed through the briars and brambles before they began baying. "They on a trail," the handler said, pushing through the brush behind his dogs. About half a mile later, the dogs arrived at the house of Dolphus Ross, a fifty-year-old Black man. As deputies surrounded the house, Sheriff Frost ordered the people inside to come out with their hands up. Both Dolphus and his son Leroy, nineteen, came out peacefully; they were arrested, driven to town, and placed in jail.

The county jail was not only a place to incarcerate criminals but also the home of Sheriff Frost, fifty-six; his wife, Maud; and his two children, Willie, thirty, and Marsha, sixteen. Willie had followed his father into law enforcement and was working as one of his father's deputies at the time. Residing on the second floor of the jail, their life was not one of extravagance, but they saved money and Sheriff Frost was as close to his job as humanly possible. A proactive sheriff, Frost was talented at finding and destroying alcohol stills, arresting offenders, and making rounds throughout the town to check if all the businesses were safe. Being a sheriff in a small town had its advantages; it also had its downsides, as Sheriff Frost would find out when he arrested Dolphus and Leroy Ross.

Wide-eyed and worried, Dolphus and Leroy shuffled inside the jail followed by Sheriff Frost and his deputies. Stepping through the cell door, the prisoners sat on opposite sides of the room on the small beds provided for the jail's occupants while the deputies removed their cuffs. Backing out of the cell, Sheriff Frost slammed the door, which sounded to Dolphus and Leroy like a lid shutting on their coffin. Walking down the hall toward his office, Sheriff Frost sat in his desk chair, removed his hat, and ran a hand through his graying hair. If tempers in the town raged out of control, which he believed they might, this could be bad. After much thought, Sheriff Frost decided he needed to wait until the morning, when tempers cooled off, to question the prisoners.

With no other duties for the day, Sheriff Frost rose from his desk and walked up the stairs to his living quarters. After supper, certain that the prisoners would be safe, he asked Maud if she wanted to go to the moving picture show. As they had in most American cities, movies in Water Valley had become popular, and the sheriff and his wife especially liked them. Changing into his civilian clothes, he and Maud walked down the stairs and exited through the front door of the jail into the cool night air. When the movie was over, they strolled back arm in arm toward home. Drawing closer, nothing could have prepared them for the surprise that awaited them in front of the jailhouse. Anywhere from twenty-five to forty armed men stood waiting outside the jail. Despite recognizing many of the men as Cofer's relatives, Sheriff Frost did not feel more at ease.

Stepping from the crowd, a big burly man armed with a pistol demanded, "Give us the keys, Sheriff."

Straightening his back, Sheriff Frost said, "I can't do that, fellas. I suggest you all get back in your vehicles and go home. You don't want to do this."

"Are you going to be a problem?" the man asked.

Knowing that the odds were not in his favor, Sheriff Frost answered, "No, but can I least get my family out of our quarters above the jail?"

The burly man nodded, and Sheriff Frost and his wife scrambled in the front door and up the stairs. In a matter of minutes, the whole family hurtled down the stairs and headed to the courthouse to take shelter.

Once the sheriff fled, some men, armed with hammers and chisels, entered the jail. As they attacked the cell door, it soon gave way, allowing them access to the prisoners. The mob grabbed the two Black men from the cell and forced them, at gunpoint, into one of the waiting automobiles. After driving three miles east of town, the mob's anger rose to a boiling point. Stopping, they dragged the reluctant Black men out of the car and, after a heated discussion, decided to let Leroy go. As he ran into the darkness, the night was lit with gunfire and his father's body pitched forward onto the ground riddled with more than twenty bullets. A coroner's inquest determined that the cause of Dolphus's death was gunshot fired by an "unidentified" mob. Satisfied that the case was closed, there was no further investigation into the murder.

11
DENIAL

All eyes turned to look at Emmett Shaw as he stepped inside the sheriff's office. He was a small dark-skinned man of thirty-five with a neatly trimmed mustache and a receding hairline. His narrow shoulders were slumped, his dark brown eyes were glued to the floor, and unlike Sam Whitaker, there was no smile playing on his lips. Even though Shaw was cooperating, one of the deputies shoved him roughly into the small interrogation room and forced him into a chair.

Immediately, Emmett said, "I didn't have a thing to do with killing those good people."

Detective Fox found it interesting that Emmett would immediately deny any part in the murder. The guilty dog barks first, he thought.

Sheriff Doyle leaned forward and asked, "You have been on the chain gang, and they don't keep you locked up all night, can you prove where you were last night?"

Unable to answer the question, Emmett looked as if he had been slapped, but he remained firm. He had nothing to do with the murders. If he was guilty, what was his motive? After further questioning the suspect, Sheriff Doyle and Detective Fox believed that they pinpointed the motive. Having worked for W.B. as a porter in the clothing store, Emmett had been fired for petty theft and turned over to the law. According to Sam Whitaker, the hatred that he and Emmett had for W.B. and Mamie Wagner had boiled over, resulting in them plotting the murders of the rich couple.

During the interview, the investigators brought in Adele Whitaker, Sam's fifteen-year-old sister. Slightly taller than her older brother, she was dressed in a plain flowered print dress and a pair of flats. Her hair, which was cropped off close to her scalp, gave her the appearance of a young man. Unlike Emmett, she began to talk as soon as she sat down. With little prodding from the lawmen, Adele admitted that she, very poorly, had helped her brother and Emmett attempt to clean up the crime scene. Her version of events so closely matched that of her brother's that the lawmen were convinced that Sam Whitaker had told the truth.

With his knowledge of lynchings, Sheriff Doyle determined that his prisoners should be moved to another location if they wanted to live to see the dawn. Calling Sheriff Sam Coleman of Leflore County, he asked if he could move his prisoners to the Leflore County Jail in Greenwood. Sheriff Coleman agreed to the request and said he would do his best to keep Adele, Sam, and Emmett alive until their trial.

Informing Sam, Adele, and Emmett of his intentions, Sheriff Doyle secretly loaded them into a civilian car and began the hour drive to

A Mississippi chain gang like the one that Emmett Shaw was serving on hours before W.B. and Mamie Wagner were murdered. *Library of Congress.*

Greenwood. Fortunately for the lawmen, during the ride Sam began to give even more details about the murders. He told them that when he struck Mamie the first time, it knocked her across the dining room table, splattering the tablecloth with blood. To cover up his crime, he removed the tablecloth, wadded it up, and placed it in a laundry basket. Sam's mouth had sealed his, Emmett, and Adele's fate, as that piece of information had not been released to the public. Only the killer(s) would have known that the bloody tablecloth ended up in the laundry basket. With the amount of evidence found at the crime scene and Sam's and Adele's confessions, the chances of the three suspects being found guilty were astronomical.

Greenwood, Mississippi, incorporated in 1844, was named for Choctaw Chief Greenwood Leflore. Like many towns in Mississippi, Greenwood's economy was successful because it acted as a shipping point for trains running to Memphis, New Orleans, and St. Louis, until the end of the Civil War. During the War Between the States, Greenwood also served as a staging area for General Grant's troops on his way to lay siege to Vicksburg. When the war ended and the South's economy was reorganized, Greenwood experienced another boom when two new railroad lines were built through the town. During the Great Depression, the town's economy faltered, but it recovered during World War II. During the 1960s, Greenwood became an epicenter for the civil rights movement as the Student Nonviolent Coordinating Committee, Council of the Federated Organizations, and the Mississippi Freedom Democratic Party worked hard in the town trying to register Black voters during Freedom Summer.

However, on the night that Sheriff Doyle pulled into Greenwood with his three prisoners, the city's population was eleven thousand citizens. Coming to a halt in front of the jail, Sheriff Doyle removed his three prisoners from the car in rapid succession. Sheriff Coleman greeted them at the door, and despite the seriousness of the situation, the two lawmen greeted each other warmly, exchanging a firm handshake. As they guided their prisoners up the stairs to the jail, all sense of defiance or fight had left Sam Whitaker, but Emmett Shaw was still adamant that he had nothing to do with the murders.

As they entered the building, Sheriff Doyle asked, "Do you have a stenographer on staff?"

"I believe we can round one up," Sheriff Coleman said, waving for one of his deputies to come closer. "Go and get a stenographer and be quick about it."

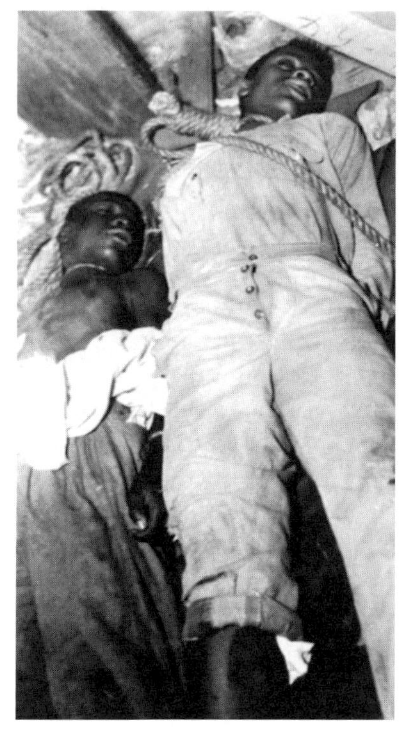

The bodies of Ernest Green (*right*) and Charlie Lang (*left*). The picture was taken at Patton's Undertaking Establishment in Shubuta, Mississippi. *Bettmann/Corbis.*

The deputy ran to his car, jumped inside, and zoomed down the road. He was gone for what seemed like an eternity, but it couldn't have been more than twenty minutes before he returned with a stenographer in tow. Rushing into the jail, equipment in hand, the stenographer set up in the small interrogation room. When she had settled in, each prisoner was brought in and asked to repeat what they had said back in Water Valley. Once the prisoners' stories were recorded, the Water Valley lawmen drove back home and began connecting every piece of evidence to the confessions.

Despite Greenwood being an hour away from Water Valley, Sheriff Coleman brought in extra deputies to watch the three prisoners. There would be no lynchings on his watch. Justice, not vigilantism, needed to prevail if Mississippi ever wanted to move away from the ghosts of the past. Unfortunately, lynching was far from over in the Magnolia State, and eleven years after the arrest of Sam Whitaker, Adele Whitaker, and Emmett Shaw, Mississippi would be propelled back into the national news with the lynching of two fourteen-year-old Black boys.

The two young men, Charlie Lang and Ernest Green, were arrested in October 1942 for the alleged assault and rape of a thirteen-year-old white girl, who had been attacked while walking home from school. Arrested and taken before the court, both boys pleaded guilty and were incarcerated in the Quitman County Jail. City Marshal G.F. Dabbs, confident that he could protect the prisoners, was put in charge of guarding the jail. Later that night, Dabbs heard a knock on the outside door, and when he went to answer it, a blanket was thrown over his head by an angry mob. Taking Marshal Dabbs's keys, the mob locked him in an empty holding cell and disappeared into the darkness with the two scared prisoners.

When news of the kidnapping spread through the county, Sheriff Lloyd McNeal of Clarke County launched a search in the early morning hours. Just a few hours after the search began, Sheriff McNeal found the bodies of the boys hanging from the old railroad bridge spanning the Chickasawhay River where the thirteen-year-old girl had been attacked. Once again, vigilante justice had prevailed in Mississippi, reaffirming the idea that Blacks were often denied the right to a fair trial.

Whether it was the fact that the boys were so young or that they were given no trial, the response to these lynchings was met by much anger from politicians in Jackson, Mississippi. Governor Paul Johnson was quoted as saying, "Every man who lynched those negroes is guilty of murder and I want the public to know that the Governor of Mississippi condemns the act and will exert every reasonable effort to see the laws of Mississippi are vindicated. Such acts are spots on the good name of Mississippi and the better class of people here that condemn the wrong." The governor later inquired about why Sheriff McNeal had not moved the prisoners after they pleaded guilty. The sheriff responded that he had been advised by the county attorney that the two prisoners would be safe if they were left in Quitman County Jail. The boys' deaths prompted the NAACP to accelerate a campaign to end lynching throughout the South and ensure that African Americans gained the right to a trial by jury.

12

WATER VALLEY AND THE GREAT DEPRESSION

As America moved out of World War I into the Roaring Twenties, many parts of the country began to prosper, but Mississippi remained a strange combination of racial tension, poverty, and the past. With the War to End All Wars over, Mississippi's cotton prices fell from forty cents a pound to nine cents, causing many Mississippi farmers, who had borrowed extra money to expand their operation during the war, to lose their farms when they failed to pay off their loans. Luckily for Mississippi, agricultural expansion for some farmers came in the form of dairy farming and dairy processing, which helped to stabilize the state's agricultural industry.

Another change that took place throughout the South and heavily affected Mississippi was the Great Migration, beginning in 1910 and lasting until 1920. During that decade, 150,000 African Americans fled Mississippi to escape racial prejudice and to find jobs in Northern factories. Between 1920 and 1940, another 150,000 African Americans left the Magnolia State, and the number continued to climb even greater when 300,000 others migrated to the North. The migrations left many parts of Mississippi scrambling for manual laborers, resulting in some of its white citizens taking drastic measures to keep African Americans from leaving. In several Mississippi towns, police entered railroad passenger cars and removed Black passengers to prevent them from departing. On the Illinois Central Railroad, the trains were often diverted by railroad workers so that they could stop the Black passengers from leaving. More determined than ever, many Black leaders used the threat of migration as a bargaining chip to achieve more equal rights in the state and throughout the South.

Water Valley was not exempt from the economic downturn, but the city had one thing that many other places didn't: the railroad. In 1922, the local newspaper ran an article about the Illinois Central Railroad's plans to extend and improve the railroad shops, which stated, "Whereas the improvements and enlarged plant mean the employment of a larger complement of laboring men, which will give lucrative employment to a large number of our citizens." The excitement surrounding the extension of the railroad was palpable as people lined up for jobs. The construction efforts were marked by a celebration on October 5, 1922, that, according to the paper, every citizen was urged to attend and enjoy. Once again, the railroad proved to be the lifeblood of Water Valley, extending its boom and helping the city reach its peak population in the early twentieth century.

As much as the railroad brought success and economic growth to Water Valley, it also brought difficulties. The year before the ICC extension, railroad lines throughout the South were prone to attacks against African American firemen who worked for the railroads. Three Black firemen had been fired on by what the paper described as an "organized" band of assassins who were attempting to scare African Americans away from working on the railroad. In Mississippi, these attacks occurred at Water Valley, Banks, and Lake Cormorant. Farther north, an attack occurred at Raines, Tennessee, also on the Illinois Central Railroad. The newspaper claimed that the assailants even fired inside the engine, endangering the Black firemen and passengers alike. Unfortunately, three Black railroad workers were killed during the attacks. Governor Lee Maurice Russell issued a statement to the press: "I am sure that this form of lawlessness will be condemned by all law-abiding citizens of this state, and I am making this public declaration to the end that all officers everywhere shall be especially vigilant in apprehending and punishing this sort of criminals." The violence on the railroads died down, but the problems faced by Mississippi's Black population were far from over.

With Mississippi having more than ten thousand dairy farms and one hundred milk plants in the state during the 1920s, W.B. Wagner once again saw an opportunity to make money when he became one of the chief stockholders in the Yalobusha Creamery Company. Like King Midas, everything that W.B. touched turned gold; he was one of several investors that received a portion of $250,000 from the creamery over a five-year period. His role in the creamery also allowed him an inside track when it came to selling his twine to dairy farms across the state.

Regardless of his good fortune, W.B. and Water Valley were dealt a blow in April 1926 when the Yocona Twine Factory burned to the ground. The fire started at 3:15 p.m. in the boiler room of the factory. As the alarm sounded, firemen and other responders rushed to the scene. Superintendent C.E. Romberger barked orders as the men ran around, desperately trying to put out the flames, but unfortunately, the wind picked up, causing the flames to soar even higher. Eventually, the firemen had no choice but to watch the factory burn to the ground. The fire destroyed seventy-five bales of lint cotton, plus $100,000 of equipment and property. The factory fire marked the loss of jobs for many people who were barely keeping their heads above water. The factory also had great historical value as one of the oldest institutions in Yalobusha County. Luckily for the owners, the damage was partially covered by insurance.

With Water Valley reeling from the loss of the twine factory, the town hoped that 1927 would be better than 1926, but they were sadly mistaken. Slowly and unfortunately for the town, the Illinois Central Railroad began to shift its traffic to the Grenada-Memphis line, bypassing Water Valley. The town suffered another huge blow when the ICR moved its maintenance facility to Kentucky. Left with no choice but to follow the work, five hundred families packed up their belongings and left Water Valley for the Blue Grass State. City businesses, including W.B.'s clothing store, experienced a drop in profits with the loss of population and the reduction of train passengers stopping in the town to shop. By 1930, the city's population had fallen to 3,738, a loss of almost 600 residents from the 1920 census.

Down on their luck, the residents of Water Valley could not have predicted what would happen on October 24, 1929. Black Tuesday, as the date is called, was the worst stock market crash in the history of the United States. Millionaires became paupers overnight, suicide rates rose by 30 percent, mental health facilities became overcrowded, and the unemployment rate soared to an unbelievable 25 percent. America's economy was in shambles, and Mississippi was not immune. Mississippi had struggled with poverty since the Civil War, and the state's farm income dropped by 64 percent from 1929 to 1933. During the late 1920s, farming in Yalobusha County took another hit when many of the cotton crops became infested with boll weevils. The boll weevil, a gray insect with a long snout, worked its way north from Mexico, and by the late 1800s, it had infected all the cotton-growing regions in the southeastern area of the United States. With the Depression in full swing and the cotton crops damaged, many farmers forfeited on their loans, losing their farms in the process.

During this time, W.B. Wagner, as the president of the Bank of Water Valley, faced a problem that he had never faced: People no longer trusted banks. With banks closing left and right, due in part to President Hoover's inactivity to help struggling financial institutions, bank deposits dropped from $101 million to $49 million from 1929 to 1933. When people were lucky enough to get money, they hid it at home; some even buried it in jars in their yard. The economic downturn also led to many people defaulting on their loans and the bank seizing their property. Bank leaders, especially those who seized property, were often considered the enemy by the public. It wasn't until President Franklin D. Roosevelt, who defeated Herbert Hoover in 1933, declared a nationwide bank holiday from March 6 to 9, 1933, that confidence in the banking system was restored.

President Roosevelt's New Deal brought more changes to Water Valley when he created the Civilian Conservation Corps, the Works Progress Administration, and the Tennessee Valley Authority. The CCC, which employed unmarried men aged eighteen to twenty-five, focused on conservation projects and led to the creation of Tishomingo State Park. The WPA employed people to construct buildings, bridges, schools, and other public projects. The TVA provided the South with not only jobs but also cheap electricity, areas of recreation, flood control, soil conservation, and even improved drinking water quality. Of course, not all of President Roosevelt's ideas were met with excitement, but those people in Water Valley who were employed by one of his federal programs were grateful for the opportunity to work.

13
A FUNERAL AND THREE TRIALS

Water Valley Presbyterian Church was standing room only for the funeral of W.B. and Mamie Wagner. Most of the people were family and friends from Water Valley, but there were also many people from out of town, some prominent members of the Mississippi government. At the front of the sanctuary, W.B.'s and Mamie's matching caskets gleamed underneath the sanctuary's lights. As Reverend O.M. Anderson stepped to the pulpit, many women in the pews were fanning themselves as the Mississippi heat crept inside the building, stifling the large crowd. When he finally did speak, Reverend Anderson's voice boomed out, extolling the accomplishments of both W.B. and Mamie. When he finished, he sat down and was replaced by Reverend J.W. Dorman and then Reverend J.D. Wrotten.

When the eulogies were over and the songs had been sung, the fourteen pallbearers rose from their seats, grabbed the two coffins by the handles, and carried them to the waiting hearses. W.B. and Mamie's last ride was a short one, less than a mile, to the Oak Hill Cemetery, where they were buried side by side. With their bodies buried, Sheriff Doyle's determination to bring their murderers to justice without a lynching was increased. Justice, Doyle believed, must be handed down in a court of law, not by an angry mob. However, the controversy surrounding the three prisoners was far from over, and at least one person was accused of trying to benefit from the threat of violence against the suspected murderers.

Born in 1907 in Memphis, Tennessee, Gerald Kelley grew up in a world of privilege. His father, Thomas, and mother, Camille, were both successful, well-paid lawyers, which is evident in the 1910 census that lists two servants as part of their household. By 1920, Camille had been promoted to serve as a judge in a juvenile court in Memphis, which provided her with a good deal of prestige among her peers and the city. Despite their lives being on track, tragedy struck the Kelley family in 1928, when Gerald's sister, twelve-year-old Evelyn, died of diphtheria. Gerald; his older brother, Heiskell; and their parents were devastated over the death of the youngest family member. Unfortunately, in the years to come, tragedy would not be in short supply for the Kelley family.

Raised in a family that esteemed the law and education, Heiskell followed in his parents' footsteps and became a lawyer. Like his older brother, Gerald graduated college but avoided law school; instead, he became a newspaper reporter at the *Memphis Press-Scimitar*. The *MPS* was created in 1926 when the *Memphis News Scimitar* and the *Memphis Press* merged. The new merger proved successful, but the paper's heyday did not start until Edward Meeman took over in late 1931. Meeman would remain the paper's editor until 1962, when he retired from the newspaper business. He died just four years later at the age of seventy-seven. Even before the Meeman era, the *MPS* was known as a newspaper that based its information on honest journalism; that is why it shocked the city of Memphis when Sheriff Doyle issued an arrest warrant for Gerald Kelley for libel.

Whether or not he had been fed misinformation, intentionally falsified information, or was telling the truth, we don't know for sure, but Gerald Kelley, shortly after the murders of W.B. and Mamie Wagner, wrote an article for the afternoon publication of the *Press-Scimitar* stating that a large, angry armed mob formed in Water Valley with the intentions of driving to Greenwood to lynch the three murder suspects. However, when the mob never showed up in Greenwood, Kelley was charged with libel. Shortly after Kelley's arrest, Littleton Upshur, editor of the *Greenwood Commonwealth* and a Greenwood businessman, posted the $1,000 bond for Kelley to be released from jail. District Attorney Milton Thompson stated that the bond would be held until the grand jury either charged Kelley or dismissed the charges against him. Appearing before the county circuit court on the morning of May 8, Kelley said, "Everything published in that story is true. I saw the things I wrote about, and I have plenty of witnesses to prove it." The grand jury eventually dismissed the charges, and Kelley went on to write for papers in Milwaukee, Buffalo, New York, and even

Asia. Eight years later, in 1939, Kelley passed away at age thirty-two from pneumonia in Boston, Massachusetts.

As May turned into June and the threat of vigilante justice faded, Emmett, Sam, and Adele fell into a routine inside the Greenwood City Jail. When they were transported to Water Valley to be indicted, Sam, Adele, and Emmett were shocked to see an army of armed guards in front of the courthouse. With their feet and ankles shackled, they eased from the car, clanking their way into the packed courthouse. With the Mississippi heat rising to almost unbearable temperatures, the courtroom's windows were wide open, and the gallery was crowded with onlookers, adding to the heat of the courtroom. Sam and Emmett shuffled their way to stand before the bench.

Peering down over the top of his glasses, Judge Greek Rice asked, "How do you plead?"

"Not guilty," the two men answered in unison. An audible groan rose from the gallery, accompanied by eye rolls and head nods.

Typing away on the stenography machine, the court reporter, showing no emotion, recorded each spoken word in shorthand to be typed later for the court transcripts. All business, the judge quickly assigned two lawyers to defend Sam and Emmett. Next, the judge ordered jurors be summoned for jury selection. Due to the brutality of the murders, the wealth of the victims, and the race of the defendants, the judge wanted to expedite the trial, setting it for June 11, the following Thursday.

After the judge had accepted the two male suspects' pleas, Adele Whitaker was escorted into the courtroom to stand before Judge Rice.

"Miss Whitaker," Judge Rice said, "do you understand the severity of the charges that stand against you?"

"Yes suh'," she said, still glancing at the floor.

"And you still wish to plead guilty to accessory to murder?" Judge Rice asked.

"Yes suh'," she said, daring not elaborate. "My brother, Sam, and Emmett Shaw made me help with the cleaning up and burying of Ms. Mamie and Mr. W.B.'s bodies. They kilt them with a butcher knife and an axe."

"Well…I have no choice but to accept your plea and I will hold your sentencing over till after the trial of your brother and Emmett Shaw," Judge Rice declared, slamming his gavel against his bench.

On Thursday, June 11, Sheriff Doyle rose from the bed, took his shaving cup and brush in hand, wet the soap, and worked the brush back and forth until it created a nice thick foam. Spreading it on his cheeks, he took his straight razor and began to move the blade carefully across his face. Staring in the mirror, he thought today could be the biggest day

The Yalobusha County Courthouse was one of the most impressive buildings in northeast Mississippi before it burned in 1912. *hillcountryhistory.org*.

of his law enforcement career. Toweling his face off, he dressed, strapped on his gun belt, and headed to his office. Some of his deputies were already there, milling around, waiting for what would be the biggest trial in the history of the town. Under Sheriff Doyle's orders, the deputies armed themselves with rifles and tear gas. Marching out of the office, they walked the short distance to the courthouse and took up their guard positions. Sheriff Doyle was determined that no one, guilty or innocent, would be lynched on his watch.

With the armed lawmen in place, fifty white male voters were escorted into the courthouse for the voir dire, the French term for "to speak the truth," a portion of the trial where the prosecutors, the defense attorneys, and the judge choose twelve suitable jurors. Once the potential jurors were inside the courthouse, the deputies followed them inside.

"All rise," the bailiff announced, causing those seated in the courtroom to stand, "for the Honorable Greek Rice."

Draped in a black robe, Judge Greek Rice cut an imposing figure as he walked up the few steps to sit on his bench. Greek Rice, whose name sounds more like a food dish than a judge, was born in Tallahatchie County, Mississippi, on May 18, 1886. The son of Lent and Annie Passgrove Rice, Greek showed an early propensity for education in the small rural county schools. Graduating from high school, Rice headed to Clinton, Mississippi, to attend Mississippi College in 1908, where he received his undergraduate degree. Longing to practice law, Rice attended Cumberland College in Lebanon, Tennessee, where he earned a law degree in 1911. Passing the Mississippi Bar, Rice hung his shingle out in Charleston, Mississippi. When an opportunity to move and practice in Washington, D.C., presented itself, Rice moved north and worked in the alien property custodian office from 1918 to 1919.

Longing for a career in politics, Rice moved back to the Magnolia State and campaigned for a seat in the Mississippi House of Representatives, which ended successfully with him being elected in 1920. Despite campaigning hard and loving politics in Jackson, an opportunity arose in 1921 that he could not pass up, so he resigned from the House of Representatives and accepted a seat on the bench as Mississippi's Seventeenth District circuit court judge. This was the position he was serving in when Sam, Emmett, and Adele appeared before his bench in June 1931. With newspapers across the state carrying articles about Water Valley's most famous trial, Judge Greek Rice became a household name. In August 1931, following the Wagner trial, Judge Rice, spurred on by his publicity, ran for the office of Mississippi attorney general and won. He held the position for eighteen years, dying in office on February 21, 1950, at the age of sixty-three.

When both the prosecutor and the defense had agreed on a twelve-man jury, Judge Rice determined that there was enough time left before lunch to proceed with the trial. After the opening statements of the prosecutor and defense attorney, the prosecutor, who had the burden of proof, began calling witnesses to the stand.

"Mr. Thompson, call your first witness," Judge Rice ordered.

Rising from the prosecution table, Thompson said, "The state calls Callie Wiggins to the stand."

The people in the gallery turned to see Callie Wiggins, eyes cast down, not glancing left or right, as she placed her hand on the Bible and swore to tell the whole truth before she sat down in a chair to the right of the judge.

Shoving his hands deep in his pockets, Thompson walked to stand next to Wiggins. "Can you state your name and where you live?"

"Yes suh'. My name is Callie Wiggins. I live in Water Valley, on Lee Street, house number 206."

"And were you employed by W.B. and Mamie Wagner at the time of their murders?"

"Yes suh'," she said.

"And what did you do for the Wagners?"

"I cooked, suh', and did a little house cleaning," she said.

"Can you describe the events of the morning of May 5?"

Callie Wiggins recounted her day from when she rose until the moment she walked in on the horrific scene at the Wagners' home. The most effective part of her testimony was when she recalled her interaction with Sam Whitaker that morning and how he said that there was no use going inside because W.B. and Mamie weren't home. Callie's testimony about how the normally pristine house was disheveled and covered in blood painted a grisly picture for the jury. By the time Judge Rice adjourned for lunch, the prosecutor had presented most of his evidence, including the most critical evidence: the bloody fingerprints.

After lunch, the courtroom was still packed, and the armed guards were positioned where they had been earlier that morning. With the prosecution having rested, it was now the defense attorney's turn to present evidence contrary to the prosecution's. Despite Sam Whitaker's initial detailed confession about the murder and the crime scene, they had to plant the seed of reasonable doubt into the minds of the jury. At some point during his incarceration, Sam had retracted his statement about the murder, stating that he had played no part in the deaths of W.B. and Mamie Wagner. The defense also focused on two other points: the fact that Emmett never confessed to participating in the murders and that Sam Whitaker, they believed, was mentally deficient.

Their attempts at establishing reasonable doubt were futile, and the jury deliberated for just eleven minutes before returning a guilty verdict. With a guilty verdict hanging over Sam's head, there was no sign of the brash young teenager as he was led away in shackles back to Yalobusha County Jail. Emmett Shaw's trial was up next.

14

GUILTY OR NOT GUILTY

On Friday, June 12, the courtroom was packed again for the trial of Emmett Shaw. Regardless of the peaceful nature of Sam Whitaker's trial, armed guards were standing in the same spot as they did the day before. Despite taking great precautions, Sheriff Doyle told the press that the citizens of Water Valley were peaceable people and that there should be no issue with violence during or after the trial.

Quiet spread across the courtroom as Emmett, shackled hand and foot, shuffled into the courtroom, his eyes trained on the floor. He had not glanced at the crowd, but every eye in the building was now fixed on him as he sat at the defense table. With the jury returning a guilty verdict against Sam Whitaker in under eleven minutes, Emmett's chances of being found not guilty were slim to none.

"All rise for the Honorable Greek Rice," the bailiff said, his voice carrying through the small courtroom.

Judge Rice appeared in his black robe, the same solemn expression on his face from the day before. Wanting to be sure everything was done by the book, he gave the jury a few last-minute instructions before he told District Attorney Milton Thompson to present his case.

District Attorney Milton Thompson, sixty years old at the time of the trial, was born in January 1871 to James Polk Thompson, a farmer, and Alice Thompson, a housewife, in Tate County, Mississippi. Growing up a farmer's son, there is no doubt that Milton, along with his four siblings, did their fair share of manual labor to help on their small farm.

Determined not to work on the farm for the rest of his life, Thompson sought an education, and his occupation was listed as teacher in the 1900 census. Between 1900 and 1910, Thompson studied for and passed the Mississippi Bar Exam, practicing privately before deciding to go into the public arena. Before running for district attorney, Thompson served as Tate County attorney for the board, county prosecutor, attorney clerk, and chancery clerk. During his bid for the Office of District Attorney of Mississippi's Seventeenth Judicial District, his numerous supporters paid for several ads in the *Sun-Sentinel* on August 18, 1927, that sang Thompson's praises. During the primary, Thompson defeated his opponents by 2,089 votes to 247. Milton went on to win the final election by a wide margin. When he reached the trials of Sam and Adele Whitaker and Emmett Shaw, Milton Thompson had been practicing law for longer than the two younger defendants had been alive.

Milton Thompson wasted no time in calling Sam Whitaker to the stand to testify against Emmett Shaw. Whether it was because he had already been found guilty or he believed that his testimony might help reduce his sentence, Sam seemed more relaxed than he had been during his trial.

"Mr. Whitaker, can you tell us what happened the day of the murder?" Milton asked.

"Yes suh', me and Emmett had planned to kill them and that's what we did," Sam said, shifting in his seat.

"Can you tell the court why you and Emmett Shaw killed them?"

"I wanted to kill 'em because Mr. W.B. threatened to whip me 'cause I hadn't brought back his gun. Emmett wanted to kill 'em because when he was arrested for theft, Mr. W.B. wouldn't pay his fine."

"Why was it important for Mr. W.B. to pay his fine?" Thompson asked, glancing at the jury.

"If Mr. WB. had paid his fine then he wouldn't have had to work on that chain gang. Emmett hated working on that chain gang."

"Thank you, Sam. You are dismissed."

During the next few hours, Milton Thompson presented the same evidence and witnesses as he had in the first trial. Finally, he rested, leaving the rest of the trial to Kermit Cofer, Emmett's defense attorney.

At twenty-two years old, Kermit Roosevelt Cofer was hoping to make a name for himself in the trial of the century in Water Valley. Born on September 28, 1908, to John Wilson Cofer and Frances Catherine Hughes, he was the youngest of eight children. Both his parents and all eight children labored on their small farm as he grew up. Cofer, who was not inclined to the profession of farming, enrolled at the University of Mississippi, where he received a degree in jurisprudence. After hanging out his shingle in Water Valley, he determined to help represent even the clients who could not afford his fees.

With the evidence heavily stacked against his client, Cofer was determined to focus on the one constant that Emmett Shaw had going for him: his continued denials of guilt. Calling witness after witness to the stand, Kermit continued to ask the same questions: "Did Emmett Shaw ever confess to participating in the murder? Did Emmett Shaw tell you he was innocent? Did Emmett Shaw deny his part in these murders?"

Each witness agreed that Emmett Shaw professed his innocence from the very beginning, but in their opinion he was guilty. When the defense rested, the jury was instructed to return to the jury room and decide Emmett's fate.

During most trials, the people in the galley would have left, returning for the verdict several hours or even days later; however, with the jury deliberation having been so quick in Sam's trial, most people just stayed seated and waited to see what happened. The decision was a good one: this time, the jury deliberated for only seven minutes before reaching a verdict.

Once again, silence fell over the courtroom as the bailiff took a piece of paper from the jury foreman, walked it over to Judge Rice, and handed it to him. Unfolding the paper, Judge Rice studied it a moment before handing it back to the bailiff, who then gave it to the foreman.

"Will the defendant please rise," Judge Rice said.

Rising from his seat, Emmett Shaw looked defeated even before the verdict was read.

"How does the jury find in the case of *The State of Mississippi versus Emmett Shaw*?" Judge Rice asked.

Opening the paper, the foreman glanced at the scribbled verdict before saying, "We find the defendant guilty."

There was an audible ripple of approval through the courtroom. Emmett Shaw's knees turned to water, and he fell backward into his chair.

Banging his gavel against his bench, Judge Rice brought the courtroom back to order before saying, "Sentencing will take place tomorrow for all three defendants. The court is dismissed."

The morning of the thirteenth, Water Valley was alive with speculation about what sentences Judge Rice would impose on the defendants. Under the law, both Emmett Shaw and Sam Whitaker would carry mandatory death sentences—how much time would Adele Whitaker receive?

Once again, the courtroom was packed as Judge Rice made his way to the bench. All heads turned to watch as Sam, Emmett, and Adele were escorted in chains to the front of the courtroom.

Clearing his throat, Judge Rice said, "Sam Whitaker and Emmett Shaw, having been found guilty of the murder of W.B. and Mamie Wagner, I now sentence you to death. On July 17, you are to be hung by the neck until dead."

Both Emmett's and Sam's knees seemed to buckle as their sentence was read aloud—death in a month and four days. Sam would never see his nineteenth birthday, and Emmett would never see his children grow up.

"As in the case of Adele Whitaker, who has already pled guilty to accessory to murder, she was sentenced to five years in the state penitentiary at Parchman. Sheriff Doyle…"

"Yes, your honor," Sheriff Doyle said.

"No one is to leave the courtroom until the charged are safely outside the courthouse and being escorted back to jail."

"Yes sir," Sheriff Doyle said, nodding for his deputies to escort the three convicts outside.

As soon as they were out the back door, people rushed to shake Milton Thompson's hand and pat him on the back. Kermit Cofer, on the other hand, gathered up his papers and made his way outside into the heat of the day. Cofer's career in law was far from over, as he spent many years working as a lawyer in Water Valley and then serving as a chancery court judge. At the pinnacle of his career, he was appointed as a justice on the Mississippi Supreme Court.

15
EXECUTIONS

Almost as soon as people began to settle in the Mississippi Territory, there was a need for a prison to house felons. The first recorded prison in Mississippi was built in Natchez in 1789. The prison housed felons, many of whom preyed on travelers along the Mississippi River and the Natchez Trace. The first state penitentiary, dubbed the Walls, was built in 1840. The construction of the Walls prison cost the state $75,000, and when completed, it housed up to two hundred inmates. With Mississippi being the Cotton Capital of the World, prison officials quickly shifted incarceration-only prisons to labor camp prisons, which forced the inmates to pick cotton, construct bales, and make hemp rope and other agricultural products. In the early 1860s, with the Civil War raging, state officials began to pardon prisoners when the Confederate army was in desperate need of soldiers. After the war, Mississippi experienced a rise in crime and violence, which led to a need for an even larger prison system. There was no state penitentiary as such, but the Mississippi State Legislature agreed in the late nineteenth century that it hoped to solve that problem.

The overlying question was whether to build a traditional cellblock prison or rely on the penal farm system. With financial statements in hand, prison officials and other experts testified before the Mississippi legislature about how the traditional cellblock system was expensive and provided less of a chance for rehabilitation. Penal colonies, on the other hand, were cheaper to construct and would generate income for the prison system, keep prisoners busy, and teach them valuable job skills that could be used outside if they were ever released. In 1901, with the type of prison system determined, the legislature appropriated $80,000 to purchase the 3,789-acre Parchman Plantation in Sunflower County. The county, named for the Sunflower River, which flows through the county, was formed in February 1844 in the Mississippi Delta. Due to the rich, dark delta soil, Sunflower and Bolivar Counties, during the antebellum period, produced more cotton than any other counties in Mississippi. With the growth of cotton being the main industry in the state, the number of slaves in 1860 outnumbered white residents by 76,099.

The Mississippi legislature continued to purchase land in the Delta, acquiring twenty-three thousand more acres, fourteen thousand acres of which would be used for Parchman Farm. In 1901, four stockades were constructed for prisoners, who were ordered to clear the land so that prison construction could begin. The single-story lumber and brick buildings, known as "cages," were built by the convicts themselves. In 1905, Parchman's first official year of operation began with inmates working ten to fifteen hours a day, six days a week, plowing, planting, hoeing, and picking cotton. The conditions of the Mississippi Delta were harsh, as temperatures soared into the mid-nineties. Diseases such as tuberculosis, malaria, yellow fever, and others were rampant, ending many inmates' lives prematurely. At the end of 1902, Parchman earned $185,000 for the state, making it one of the most profitable government institutions in the Southeast.

In Parchman, punishments for bad behavior were often harsh, and if their behavior was bad enough, the prisoners were beaten with a whip named "Black Annie." Strangely enough, in the Jim Crow segregated Mississippi, Parchman held both Black and white, men and women. Under the stringent Jim Crow law, Parchman officials made sure to keep the white and Black inmates in segregated units. As the prison grew, it added a sawmill, cotton gin, brickyard, canning plant, and slaughterhouse. If inmates were deemed trustworthy, they were placed on the shooting squads. The "shooters," as they were called, were often mounted on horseback to ride through the acres of cottonfields acting as a deterrent for possible escapees. If a prisoner ran, the "shooters" were to shoot to kill, as was proven in August 1931 when three Black inmates, who were gathering wood for the upcoming winter, made a break for it, disappearing into the underbrush. Spotting the three inmates, Joe Blackwell, a trustee shooter who was serving a life sentence, shot and killed Velma Green. John Herbert, another trustee guard, ran down the

A group of prisoners tending crops in the early 1900s at Parchman Prison. *PBS News.*

hill and captured John Kelly, a prisoner from Tunica. The third prisoner, James Foster, slipped away into the woods. Because of their help during the jailbreak, Blackwell and Herbert were pardoned by the governor for "meritorious service."

By the time Adele Whitaker reached Parchman in 1931, there were seventeen different camps spread across the large acreage. That same year, Parchman and other state prisons were bursting at the seams from the Mississippi criminal courts prosecuting and convicting a record number of felony cases. Just before Christmas in 1931, Governor Theodore Bilbo pardoned 536 prisoners at one time, hoping that they would return to society as changed men and women. With the number of prisoners still high, many prison officials offered early release in return for good behavior. This new policy gave Adele Whitaker even more reason to keep her head down, work hard, and try not to start any trouble.

While Adele was beginning her prison term, Sam Whitaker and Emmett Shaw were in Lafayette's jail, waiting to be hanged. The July heat must have been unbearable as the two men sat in the cells dwelling on their impending deaths. With time to think, men can drive themselves crazy with the possibilities of what might have been. Regardless of how they spent their days, the two resigned themselves to their fate and made no jailbreak attempts.

Between 1921 and 1964, justice in the Magnolia State was swift: 173 men were executed for various crimes. Today, the average death row inmate in Mississippi will spend ten to twenty years on death row before being executed. Sam Whitaker and Emmett Shaw had only thirty-four days between their sentencing and their trip to the gallows, which was the preferred method of execution in the state until 1940. In 1940, the state of Mississippi welcomed the electric chair as the favored method of execution.

With the state penitentiary located in Sunflower County, the residents of the county protested the idea of having all the state's executions at Parchman, because they were worried that Sunflower County would become known as the "death capital of the state." To avoid that misnomer, Mississippi proposed an unusual solution, a portable electric chair they dubbed "Old Sparky." Old Sparky was first used on January 11, 1940, to execute twenty-eight-year-old Willie Mae Bragg, who had been convicted of killing his wife. Thanks to Old Sparky, he was executed in Jefferson Davis County, the county in which his crime had been committed. Mississippi would eventually replace the electric chair with the gas chamber in 1955 and then lethal injection, which is still in use today.

With the gallows inside the Water Valley Jail having not been used in years, Sheriff C.T. Doyle and his deputies started repairing them on July 10, a week before the hangings. There were some questions about whether the hangings should take place outside of Water Valley; however, the county supervisors determined that justice needed to be handed down in the same city where the murders had taken place. With the hangings taking place inside the jail, the executions would be closed to the public. The only witnesses to the hangings would be Sheriff Doyle, who would be pulling the trapdoor; the county coroner; some sheriff deputies; two ministers; the jailer; and some county supervisors.

On the morning of July 17, 1931, the heat was almost unbearable as a large crowd gathered around the Water Valley Jail to make sure the executions went as planned. The crowd, consisting of mostly men, stood smoking and spitting streams of tobacco juice onto the lawn as they listened for the creaking of the trapdoor to fall. Sam Whitaker was the first to step on the trapdoor and have a noose slipped onto his neck and tightened. If the knot had been tied correctly, it would break his neck, causing instant death. A "hangman's fracture," as it is called, is a break between the neck and head that snaps the cervical spine. When the rope was secured, a deputy nodded to Sheriff Doyle, who sprung the trapdoor, sending Sam Whitaker's small body spiraling downward. Stepping forward, the coroner pressed his stethoscope against Sam's chest and listened carefully. No heartbeat; the eighteen-year-old was dead. Emmett Shaw, who had professed his innocence repeatedly, was quietly escorted onto the trapdoor and the process was repeated. Their bodies were taken away without incident and buried on private property outside the city limits.

16

LIFE RETURNS TO NORMAL

With the executions over, Water Valley returned to the struggles of everyday life. The town leaders asked themselves, "How do we keep our town viable?" On August 11, 1931, the newly formed Junior Chamber of Commerce met to devise an idea to attract visitors to the struggling town. Strangely enough, with most major crops failing around Water Valley that year, there was a bumper crop of watermelons. With that in mind, the JCC decided they would hold a Watermelon Carnival on August 27, which they hoped would attract thousands of visitors from all over North Mississippi.

The JCC's first order of business would be to choose a Watermelon Queen for the festival. After much consideration, they decided on Eleanor Houston, the twenty-one-year-old daughter of Mr. and Mrs. L.S. Houston. As queen, she and the other selected maids would help preside over the festivities, making sure the carnival went smoothly. When Thursday the twenty-seventh dawned, the organizers held their breath, hoping people would pour into the town, spending their money freely. They did not have to wait long, as car after car continued to drive into town, filled with families hoping, if just for one day, to take their mind off the Depression. By the end of the day, an estimated twelve to twenty thousand people had taken part in the first Watermelon Carnival. That night, the festivities ended with a street dance and fireworks. For the next nine years, the Watermelon Carnival became a staple event for North Mississippi, but when World War II broke out, it was put on hold. Resurrected in 1980, the Watermelon Carnival is now a popular event that lasts a whole weekend in August.

During World War II, many men in Water Valley, like other small towns throughout the South, willingly joined the armed services, eager to do their part in defeating the Axis powers. During the war, Mississippi was well represented by 237,000 soldiers, more than 10 percent of the state's population. As difficult and horrible as the war was, it was a financial windfall

The 1938 Watermelon Queen, Elizabeth Caufield (*left*), and Miss Water Valley Kathleen Hague. *Water Valley Historical Society.*

for many people who had been unemployed because of the Depression. Due to increased demand, Mississippi built thirty-six new airfields and several training bases, which provided people with steady work and good wages. As the men left to fight in Europe and Asia, many women stepped out of their traditional roles, making their way to the factories to fill the void made by the men being overseas.

As the war ended in 1945, Water Valley's surviving soldiers returned home to start their lives, which had been put on hold for four years. Unfortunately, many veterans who suffered from "shell shock," now known as PTSD, had trouble readjusting to life at home. Some married women, who had been making the major decisions for their household, found it difficult to return to the more traditional role of wife and mother that had existed before World War II. Because of these differences, America's divorce rate was on the rise.

Many of the Black soldiers returned home with joy in their hearts that the war was over but a bitter taste in their mouths: Regardless of their sacrifices, they were still denied basic civil rights. Black Americans, fired up by their sacrifice during those four long years, became resolved to fight for their rights at home, and it wasn't long before they were organizing for the cause. Membership in the Southern Christian Leadership Conference, founded by Martin Luther King Jr. and other civil rights leaders, skyrocketed in the South. The NAACP and the SCLC had strong chapters in Water Valley and throughout Yalobusha County.

Unfortunately, in 1958, another incident of racial violence took place in Water Valley, inspiring the NAACP to work even harder to achieve justice and equality. It was a hot, balmy June night when Woodrow Wilson Daniels, a Black deliveryman, husband, and father of five, was pulled over for allegedly drinking while driving. James "Buster" Treloar, sheriff of Yalobusha County, initiated the stop and pulled Daniels from his car. According to a Department of Justice memo, Sheriff Treloar beat Daniels with a Billy club at the traffic stop and once again when they reached the jail. Whether he believed he went too far or Daniels was threatening to tell someone he suffered abuse, we are not sure, but Sheriff Treloar called a doctor later that night to examine the prisoner. The doctor gave Daniels a painkiller and was stunned when the sheriff began kicking his prisoner during the medical exam.

Released the next day, Daniels suffered a bloody nose and a badly swollen face. His symptoms continued to worsen, causing his family to take him to a hospital in Memphis, Tennessee, where he died a week later. One of the doctors at the hospital stated that Daniels died from severe brain trauma due to a fractured skull, which caused his brain to hemorrhage. In July 1958, Sheriff Buster Treloar was indicted on manslaughter charges. During the trial, Sheriff Treloar said he had hit Daniels, but he did not strike him on the head. When asked how he believed that Daniels's head had been hurt, Treloar said, "Must have been from an unrelated fall." The all-white jury deliberated for thirty minutes before they acquitted the sheriff, who picked up his nightstick and strolled out of the courthouse.

By 1960, the civil rights movement was burning through the South like wildfire. With sit-ins, marches, boycotts, and voter registration drives, the movement began to gain traction, and integration would slowly come to the Magnolia State. Despite the ruling of *Brown v. Board of Education*, which ruled that schools should be integrated, the South, including Water Valley, did everything it could to keep the races separate. Finally, in 1970, Water Valley complied with the federal ruling by integrating Davidson School, an all-Black school before integration, and changing its name to Water Valley Elementary School. The old Davidson School was used until 1982, when the city built a new elementary school at a different location. Unfortunately, in 1982 the old Davidson School building caught fire and burned to the ground. Some of the people in Water Valley believed that the building was a victim of arson, but the cause of the fire has never been determined.

On April 21, 1984, the clouds above Water Valley darkened, the wind picked up, and lightning pierced the sky. During the spring, these conditions aren't unusual in the South, but they could spell trouble if the clouds morph into a funnel cloud. When the sirens sounded, many residents in Water Valley scrambled for their storm houses, some took shelter in closets, some in their bathtubs, and others stayed put, believing that the weather would, as it had many times, pass over with no major consequences. Unfortunately, this time, that wasn't to be the case.

Police Chief John Watson, who was at the National Guard Armory, shouted, "Sound the sirens again." The sirens blared again but for only three minutes before the storm knocked out the power.

As the sister twisters bore down on the town, debris from nearby homes could be seen swirling amid the tornadoes. Tommy White, a Water Valley businessman, said in an interview in 1990, "The tornado sounded exactly as they had always described it, like a hundred thousand freight trains coming down the track." It was just before five thirty in the afternoon that the tornado began to chew its way through the town, touching down near Prospect Drive and Dupuy Street. Moving quickly, it struck the First

Baptist Church complex where Reverend Guy Reedy was hunkered down. As he was lifted off the ground, Reedy grabbed the door handles of the sanctuary and held on for dear life. The tornadoes then hit North Central Street hard, demolishing six businesses. In some areas, the storm left a quarter-mile-wide path of destruction. The tornado remained on the ground for five miles, causing $24 million worth of damage to the town, killing seven people, and wounding dozens of others. It was a night of terror the citizens would never forget.

Despite the disappearance of the railroad from Water Valley and the destruction of the tornadoes, the town's population in 2023 was 3,381 residents. Today, Water Valley is still a tourist destination where people step back in time by touring the Casey Jones Railroad Museum, stopping by Turnage Drugstore or Hendrick's Machine Shop, and viewing the many historical homes scattered throughout the town. Tourists often stroll along Main Street, shopping, eating, and reminiscing about simpler times. However, as peaceful as the town is today, the memory of the horror of May 5, 1931, still hangs over Water Valley.

BIBLIOGRAPHY

American Battlefield Trust. "Battle of Shiloh Facts & Summary." www.battlefields.org.

Ancestry. "1940 United States Federal Census." www.ancestry.com.

Blanco, Juan Ignacio. "Executions in Mississippi—1921–1964." DeathPenaltyUSA, the Database of Executions in the United States. https://deathpenaltyusa.org.

Brown, Brittany. "'Life Is Different Here Than It Was When I Grew Up': The Legacy of School Segregation in Yalobusha County." *Mississippi Today*, December 27, 2024. https://mississippitoday.org.

Cartmell, Donald. *The Civil War Book of Lists*. New Page Books, 2001.

Chattanooga (TN) Daily Times. "Two Negroes Hanged for Murder of Couple." July 18, 1931.

Cheng, Maria. "Hangings Are Meant to Kill Efficiently." *NBC News*, January 15, 2007. www.nbcnews.com.

City Itemizer (Water Valley, MS). January 8, 1914.

Clavin, Tom. "Mississippi Murder Mystery." *The History Reader*, May 22, 2023. www.thehistoryreader.com.

Coffeeville Scrapbook. "Early History." www.coffeevillescrapbook.com.

Daily Ardmoreite (Ardmore, OK). "Two Negroes Held for Double Killing." May 6, 1931.

DiRienzo, Daniella. "The Worst Murders in Mississippi History." Only In Mississippi. www.onlyinyourstate.com.

Evening Star (Washington, D.C.). May 1, 1951. https://www.loc.gov/collections/chronicling-america.

Facebook. "Water Valley, Ms Historical Preservation." www.facebook.com.

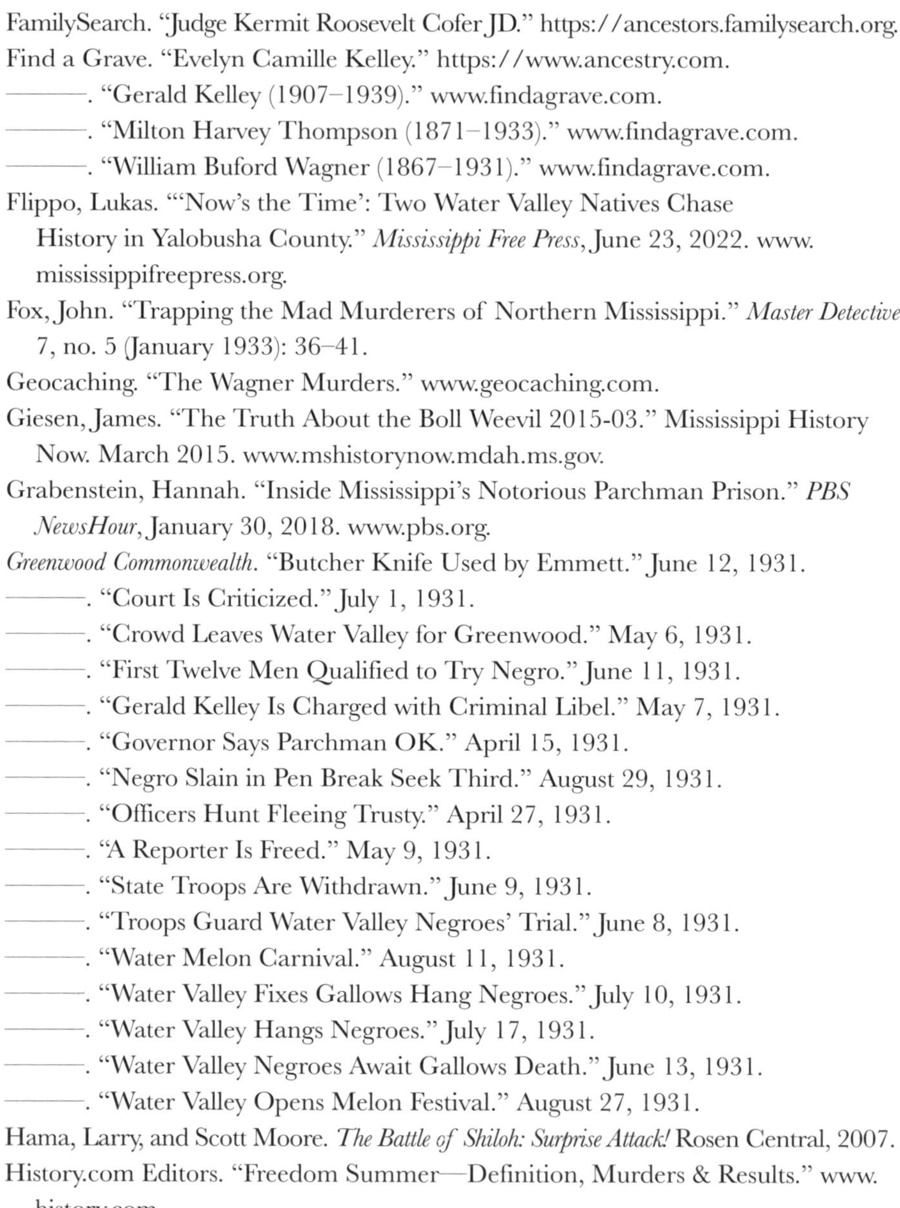

FamilySearch. "Judge Kermit Roosevelt Cofer JD." https://ancestors.familysearch.org.

Find a Grave. "Evelyn Camille Kelley." https://www.ancestry.com.

———. "Gerald Kelley (1907–1939)." www.findagrave.com.

———. "Milton Harvey Thompson (1871–1933)." www.findagrave.com.

———. "William Buford Wagner (1867–1931)." www.findagrave.com.

Flippo, Lukas. "'Now's the Time': Two Water Valley Natives Chase History in Yalobusha County." *Mississippi Free Press*, June 23, 2022. www.mississippifreepress.org.

Fox, John. "Trapping the Mad Murderers of Northern Mississippi." *Master Detective* 7, no. 5 (January 1933): 36–41.

Geocaching. "The Wagner Murders." www.geocaching.com.

Giesen, James. "The Truth About the Boll Weevil 2015-03." Mississippi History Now. March 2015. www.mshistorynow.mdah.ms.gov.

Grabenstein, Hannah. "Inside Mississippi's Notorious Parchman Prison." *PBS NewsHour*, January 30, 2018. www.pbs.org.

Greenwood Commonwealth. "Butcher Knife Used by Emmett." June 12, 1931.

———. "Court Is Criticized." July 1, 1931.

———. "Crowd Leaves Water Valley for Greenwood." May 6, 1931.

———. "First Twelve Men Qualified to Try Negro." June 11, 1931.

———. "Gerald Kelley Is Charged with Criminal Libel." May 7, 1931.

———. "Governor Says Parchman OK." April 15, 1931.

———. "Negro Slain in Pen Break Seek Third." August 29, 1931.

———. "Officers Hunt Fleeing Trusty." April 27, 1931.

———. "A Reporter Is Freed." May 9, 1931.

———. "State Troops Are Withdrawn." June 9, 1931.

———. "Troops Guard Water Valley Negroes' Trial." June 8, 1931.

———. "Water Melon Carnival." August 11, 1931.

———. "Water Valley Fixes Gallows Hang Negroes." July 10, 1931.

———. "Water Valley Hangs Negroes." July 17, 1931.

———. "Water Valley Negroes Await Gallows Death." June 13, 1931.

———. "Water Valley Opens Melon Festival." August 27, 1931.

Hama, Larry, and Scott Moore. *The Battle of Shiloh: Surprise Attack!* Rosen Central, 2007.

History.com Editors. "Freedom Summer—Definition, Murders & Results." www.history.com.

Innocence Staff. "The Lasting Legacy of Parchman Farm, the Prison Modeled After a Slave Plantation." Innocence Project. https://innocenceproject.org.

Kellum, Jacki. "Early Railroad History in Mississippi—When Water Valley Was a Hub." https://jackikellum.com.

Knecht, Phillip. "Wagner House (1890)." *Hill Country History*, March 13, 2018. https://hillcountryhistory.org.

———. "Water Valley (1858)." *Hill Country History*, March 12, 2018. https://hillcountryhistory.org.

Knoxville News-Sentinel. "Doom 2 Negroes in Mississippi." June 13, 1931.

Leathers, Laura Lee. "Water Valley: Experience the Hospitality of a Historical Railroad Town." *Magnolia Tribune*, June 22, 2023. https://magnoliatribune.com.

Mckee, Jesse O., et al. *Mississippi: The Magnolia State*. Clairmont Press, 2005.

Miami-News Record. "Writer Prosecuted for Story of Mob." May 8, 1931.

Mississippi Department of Archives & History. "Civil War Records of Yalobusha County, Roster of Water Valley Rifles, Battles and Skirmishes in Which the Company Was Engaged, List of Killed and Wounded in Battle, Summary." https://da.mdah.ms.gov.

Mississippi Department of Corrections. "A Brief History of MDOC." www.mdoc.ms.gov.

Mississippi State University. "I.C.R.P. (Illinois Central Railroad) Yards, Leading to Shops, Water Valley, Mississippi." *Scholars Junction*. https://scholarsjunction.msstate.edu.

Mitchell, Dennis J. *A New History of Mississippi*. University Press of Mississippi, 2014.

Museum of Mississippi History. "Bridging Hardship: Great Depression, New Deal, and World War II 1928–1948." https://mmh.mdah.ms.gov.

NAACP. "History of Lynching in America." https://naacp.org.

Nashville Banner. "Negroes to Die for Ax Murders." June 13, 1931.

National Park Service. "Battle Unit Details—The Civil War (U.S. National Park Service)." www.nps.gov.

———. "Soldier Details: Wagner, Daniel R." https://www.nps.gov.

National Register of Historic Places Registration Form. https://www.nps.gov.

News-Review. "Gallows Claims Three Murderers." June 18, 1931.

North Mississippi Herald (Water Valley, MS). August 17, 1923. https://www.loc.gov.

———. "The Infamous History of Water Valley." May 14, 2008. www.yalnews.com.

Oxford (MS) Eagle. "100 Years Later: The Lynching of Adolphus Ross." March 24, 2021. https://oxfordeagle.com.

Progress-Itemizer (Water Valley, MS). November 22, 1923. https://www.loc.gov.

Sun Sentinel. "Milton H. Thompson Candidate for District Attorney 17 Judicial District." August 18, 1927.

———. "Oakland." April 23, 1931.

Taylor, William Banks. *Down on Parchman Farm*. Ohio State University, 1999.

Thompson, Linda A. "A Little Bar Association History." Capital Area Bar Association. https://caba.ms.

Tulsa (OK) Tribune. "Two Negro Suspects Held for Axe Murders." May 6, 1931.
Union (MS) Appeal. "Water Valley Banker and Wife Murdered." May 7, 1931.
University of Mississippi. "Oral Histories: Black Families of Yalobusha County." https://egrove.olemiss.edu.
Water Valley Area Chamber of Commerce. "Watermelon Carnival." www.watervalleychamber.com.
Water Valley (MS) Progress. September 24, 1904. https://www.loc.gov.
Wikipedia. "Memphis Press-Scimitar." https://en.wikipedia.org.
Winona Times. "Confessed Axe Slayer Hidden by Officers." May 8, 1931.
———. "Mississippi Brevities." July 31, 1931.
Woodworth, Steven E. *Decision in the Heartland: The Civil War in the West.* Praeger, 2008.

ABOUT THE AUTHOR

Mark Neaves is a lifelong resident of northeast Mississippi. He has spent over two decades teaching history in Mississippi public schools and at the community college level. He also works as a part-time preacher, filling the pulpit when the opportunity arises. Mark graduated from Mississippi University for Women in 1999 with a bachelor's degree in social studies education. He also holds a master's degree in secondary education from the University of Mississippi and a master's in ministry from Heritage Christian University. Mark is married to Marti Neaves, his wife of twenty-five years, and they have two children, Riley and Emma Kay. He is currently still teaching history at a Mississippi public high school. He coauthored the book *Little Fish, Big Splash* and authored *Mississippi Bear Hunter Holt Collier: Guiding Teddy Roosevelt and a Lifetime of Adventure.* He hopes to continue writing for many more years.